Wake Up Oh World (WUOW)!!!!!!!

We all need to go down on inner knees
And ask that Heaven eternally forgives
From this pandemic disease
For only He dumps without environmental repercussions
No carbon emissions, warranting unsavoury demonstrations
His touch, rather, cleanses atmospheric contaminations

WUOW

Seeks ONENESS among all, for
***P**ractising **R**edeemer's **A**ttitudes **Y**ields **E**ternal **R**esults **S**acredly*
to be seen and heard

Graciously
By
Ernest Brew Obeng

ISBNs:
Paperback: 978-1-80227-241-3
eBook: 978-1-80227-242-0

Preface

Wake Up Oh World (WUOW), is for anyone who desires to find The Way to Heaven. It identifies all human as one, under sin. Loving one another irrespective, is the basic requirement of each, especially so-called believers, and worshippers. Imperative, because of how the apostles and others met JESUS. However, we have all refused this, from time immemorial, culminating in ignorantly killing those nominated to lead us. Heaven's arrival back on earth is imminent!!! How many will rejoice at this much anticipated expectation? We must become like innocent children who know no differences until ordered to avoid those we enjoyed the best times with. Agreeably, Heavenly angels come to us without any books, a clue that the word MUST be written IN individual hearts!!! They tell us what they have, which we refuse, for previous ones we still, did not listen to, in their primes, thinking we know better. Hence, always playing catch up. It demonstrates that the gap between HUMAN PERCEPTION and Heavenly reality is so huge!!!

Heavenly word is fresh, new every morning for specific purposes at specific times, to specific ones, for specific outcomes, which the Holy Books do not do!!! For example, Saul/Paul who attended a theological school, ignorantly, came out killing his very own. Whereas, Ananias, who lived in the Straight Street, did not need any human to tell him of brother Paul's coming. We, therefore, need a Heavenly encounter, to begin living Heavenly, as no man teaches Heavenly walk except the one in direct, contemporary, synchronised, daily communication. To then become innocently humble pupils, one to the other, irrespective. For, our communication is wishful thinking, a monologue!!! The "Holy Books" are good, but they do not let us communicate one-to-one with Heaven, which we all need. I need Him too!!! We must change our attitudes, first, by each seeking The Heavenly Kingdom and the accompanied righteousness, to comprehend Heavenly talk and walk. The five wise women also demonstrate that. Similarly, JESUS' apostles, who also made serious mistakes, eventually received power, thus, did not require human teachings. They led brethren to speak the TRUTH with The Heavenly accent instead of the lies that are evident in our various accents, belying our beliefs.

I have used examples from "The Bible" because I was brought up a "Christian", but stopped being one, years ago. Mortals do not serve or worship Heaven!!! We begin serving, after establishing the link through The Way of The Lord, citing again, the apostles. Here, one is uplifted among mortals in human flesh, rapture!!! WUOW also, then alerts that The Way is not studied!!! Heaven gifts that. For example, Moses was told, "go, I will talk through you." The apostles did not study from JESUS. The Holy Spirit in them directed them. This includes who we individually are, first, who JESUS is, His Father, and so on. Furthermore, JESUS' mission is completely different from theirs.

We have all approached Heaven, the wrong way, hence, the issues we face daily and centuries on end. Religion, hate, racism, tribalism, all manner of boundaries. Paper money, also, divides us into causing strife against another. All religions, beliefs and faiths are equally the same, irrespective of the perceived view, including Atheism. They are in no order of value, following, popularity or importance to Heaven!!! We must come to the point where family members are those we pass by, significantly, dealing with each, daily. We are all short of the acceptable standards for the Heavenly abode, whoever. WUOW is the world's biggest alert these days. The Heavenly accredited perfect human being, doing The Father's will, is the best book offered for Heavenly valuable humbling beginnings. WUOW, hopes to touch the world, to rethink our procedures to Heaven, including, avoiding fruitless, divisive messages and behaviours. Thus, this TRACK (Trail **R**econciling **A**ll **C**ultures **K**eenly) requires this world to move from fatal worldly attitudes and surrender wholly to The Mediator. We should adhere, believing that we can re-start, to become Heavenly children. Innocently humble, remains the most important characteristic ingredient for this epic journey. Prayer is no more a verbal demand because The Father provides in advance. For example, He said, if even we evil ones know how to provide good for our children, how much more, He, who is good, knowing, evil does no good. Hence, prayer request signifies, drifting from His canopy and insulting The Mediator, ignorantly, that He does not know what we need daily. Prayer, then, rightly, becomes a heartfelt expression of thanksgiving, for, ***P**racticing **R**edeemer's **A**ttitudes, **Y**ield **E**ternal **R**esults*. The road is extremely rough. The reward, though, beyond tops, needing a loving courage, commitment, co-ordination, agility, focus, integrity, and trust. Let us meet at the other side, knowing, The BRIDGE is set, to help us cross over, to be Heavenly awestruck.

P/S: Simon Peter, Simon Peter, for example, left his family and work to follow JESUS. He revealed the title, Christ. When others were leaving, JESUS asked Him if he was leaving too. He said no, emphatically!!! However, the same was the first and biggest anti-Christ because, among others, he denied ever knowing JESUS and took off someone's ear against JESUS' wish. Yet, he humbly accepted correction to Heaven's delight and was gracefully gifted The Holy Spirit, The Crown Jewels. This is Heaven. The rest is history, to confirm JESUS' message to him that the devil wanted to steal him, but He prayed for him. It also indicates that no matter what we think we know and do, from whosoever, without The Holy Spirit embedded in whoever, we are all ignorantly anti-Christlike, hence, not acknowledged by Heaven. Imagine, if Peter followed JESUS as the leader of the apostles, yet nearly lost everything, who are we today, world, to think we have it all readily made for us to Heaven?

Who, therefore, world, is that humble enough to be trusted with this priceless ore, called The Holy Spirit? For, including me, no one is filled with Him yet, world, be not deceived!!! We, who claim rights, with egos heightened, from the poor to the rich, anyone!!! This world is like a tennis player in a grand slam final, fifth set, 0-5 down, deuce, without the advantage, while serving at 0-40, bearing injuries to the ankle and shoulder, after a gruelling five-hour tussle!!! That dangerously, remembering that the best worldly builder refused the very piece that became the head cornerstone, ominous!!! Yet, this is the job that ONLY the one who said "I am The Way, The Truth and The Life. No one cometh onto The Father except through me", JESUS, does, with nonchalance. It is mandatory, therefore, that we get a foot in the door for any chance that may befall us. To, then, develop and demonstrate elegance that excels in Heaven.

For, the worm has turned. Heavenly rage is gathering pace. The world is listing, spinning, tossed into the air for a great fall!!! But He is ready for a worthy reconciliation. Let us do all to eliminate this perennial pandemic, sin, to then overcome all other temporary ones.

So, Wake Up Oh World, awake, to avoid the ensuing carnage, which is rushing at full throttle.

My thanks go to everyone who has been in my life in any capacity, positively for their Heavenly reward and negatively to alert me of the troughs in this complex environment. I have made many friends in, challengers, managers, colleagues, customers, cab officers, business workers, lecturers, teachers, parents, carers and not least, pupils etc. I will stop short of mentioning individual names at this stage, for the reward is on the rostrum.

Bye, ALL, for now.

Acknowledgement to My Father

Alpha and Omega, Gracious, Father in Heaven, Mr Air
Beloved Breath, readily in and out of me, without a stir
Constantly updating me of the need to stay as You dare
Developing me, in this world, far away, from the world
Ensuring my steps are daily where I can see You ahead
Forgoing everything here, remembering all ends, dread
Goodness, that lives way beyond human understanding
Humility that baffles all, with a Heavenly underpinning
Immortal, Invisible, Indomitable with Indelible writing
Just Eternal Saviour Uniquely Supreme cleanly bathing
Keen ones wanting to demonstrate You, always willing
Leadership, like none else, would adore your teachings

Master, I thank You for the treasures, only You bestow
No one but You, has the keys and codes to the controls
Omnipotent, Omnipresent, Omniscient, Greatest of old
Perfect example, for one in Heaven, on earth to behold
Quietly, doing your job, among us, with ease, and flow
Relentlessly, demonstrating a thief, with a mature pose
Sacredly ensuring that I feel You with quality attitudes
Talking truthfully to who deem You, Heavenly worthy

Unique Unassuming Lord, I desire continuing my duty
Vehemently, seeking your face, unto, foreseen eternity
Words, prayers, fasting can never redeem me infinitely
X-ray, that highlights, each mind, heart, soul, routinely

You, alone, are, my strength and shield beyond reason
Zion, reconciling even me, from nothing, to Heavenly
hero

No *number* of words, I know, Heavenly Father justifies my inclusion into The Heavenly fold. May You, therefore, accept my seeming acknowledgement, undeserved one, knowingly I am

Table of Contents

Introduction

To Heaven, we're all evil
Enjoying works of the devil
Yet, thinking in Heaven, we revel
All correlate with deceit
Displayed by deeds as receipts
Yet, wishfully thinking, Heaven, is received
Yes, all desire Heaven
Despite in evil, we're heavily laden
With none attempting removing own burden !!!

In worldly things, we innovate
Do all in it, to elevate
Strategically, aligned, we communicate
While in the Heavenly, we're dormant
With time, have turned stagnant
Eventually, now, sadly vacant
Brother against brother
Sister against sister
Religion against another

Why, no matter all efforts
We never find crumbs of comfort
Warranting Heavenly concord?
Seriously, something is wrong!!!
We want to hit The Heavenly gong
But more we try, farther away we've gone

For, all born with a void
So, of Heavenly ability, devoid
Requiring therefore Heavenly Innovative Android
Yes, all formed with a void !!!
However, devil's den, we can avoid
By refusing being employed !!!
Broken link means, all hollow !!!
No good, able to follow
So, in Heavenly demands, we don't wallow
Therefore needing answers, words, active consolation
Seeking inner joy, inspirational motivation
Yet, worsened by source and destination

We all need to go down on inner knees
And ask that Heaven eternally forgives
From this pandemic disease
For the intervention of The Sin Bearer's
Hoofing, from death barriers
Into Sacred Heavenly frontiers
So, each, reconnect the broken Seal!!!
Heaven's Foundational Deed, no one steals
The Eternal Intangible Steel, The Crown Jewels
Yes, the acknowledgement of The Heavenly Royal Assent
To start speaking TRUTH, with The Heavenly accent
Before finally, from this body, to Heaven, ascend

CHAPTER ONE

The Goal

All have sinned and fallen short of the glory of God !!!
The view of The Heavens, our Lord
How do we, this conundrum, truly resolve?
Having all messed up, without The Shepherd
From Heaven to this dying place called world
With wicked behaviours, exposing our dirt
Needing to ensure, leaving humble footprints
That, which identifies sacred DNA and finger prints
In line with Heavenly mandatory Blueprint
As our worldly innovation leaps before it looks
Religion, too, evidently, Heaven, cannot deduce
The so-called rich, with happiness, not in tune
Sadly, we have refused accepting this statement
By some insane spinning, around this pronouncement
Therefore, plunging us into unconscious retirement
There is none righteous, no, not one in communication
No one good enough, at defying this revelation
None qualifies, to defeat Heaven, in affirmation
But, trying, to prove, we are better than this recitation

Yet, without a stamp to overturn Heaven's declaration
Any humble enough one, to admit the pathetic presentation?

None jumping an inch high, when qualification, five feet
All we have, active, rubbish uttering beaks
Being so weak, leading into murky, dangerous deeps
Heaven includes all regions, race and religion
No omission regarding colour, creed or commission
All require going Heavenly, for appreciation
Instead of talking Heavenly, without aligned foundation
Good words, without substance, in operations
Without realising basic wrong, in exacerbations
Bearing religious, angelic names, even worse
Showing to Heaven, we are only, imposters
Not producing quality akin to Heaven, terse
Should therefore, take long, deep breaths
For, adrenalin, over-pumping, to untimely deaths
No escaping this, fragile and cornered
Heaven will not just make an assertion!!!
Over generations and time, then, proclamation!!!
About time, we embraced this articulation
Living as though, we know all about Heaven
Fervently, educating others too, in our salvation
Needing radical revamp in expounding
Yes, everyone fearfully, wonderfully made
But, lost, with religious leaders, doctors, unable to retrace
Hence, all, requiring humility, regaining Heavenly lane
Original characteristic image of God, gone
Now, devilish image, unacceptably, donned
Who, sacrifices what, for Heaven to re-join?

Traditions, celebrations, to Heaven, doesn't resonate
Titles, holy practices, Heaven, does not associate
Sacrifices, prayers, thanksgivings, all, Heaven alienate
For, not **Seeking**, The Heavenly Kingdom
Rather, trending, anti, The Kingdom, we have conned
Producing, on reflection, incriminating discord
The order, is to **Ye**, each of us, individually
So, inclined to be in vogue, fatal anomaly
Who, though, knows, without Heavenly humility?
We are required to diligently search, **First**
Sadly, most think we have enough, searched
Without realizing until late, that it is goalless
All assume, likes of Abraham, only a dream
But, is the level required, now, to Heavenly achieve
Which, therefore, no religion does fractionally, yield
We should humbly adhere, by changing, utterance
Slowly, alert in diverting divulgence
Delighting Heaven, with tasty evidence

The goal is for all, to move from sub-zero to positive spirituality
For now, no one immune, from Heavenly atrocity
For, even not knowing, next five minutes Heavenly activity
Each, should be in tandem with The Heavens
Gradually removing fatal burdens
Achieved only through direct Heavenly lessons
All exemplary ones found trampled on, used this route
Denying themselves, everything that worldly shoots
Throwing away, therefore, the accepted, tasty fruits
Each should stand alone, boldly
For, reckoning day, would be adjudged individually

So, should each, take bold steps, mandatory
Solely, about each living life, to write own destiny
Communicating life, with Heaven, without earthly entity
To distract, thinking, it leads to life eternity
Yes, loving The Lord The God in truth
Especially, loving neighbour as self, with proof
Finding the latter, requires more humility, to accrue
Yes, finding Heavenly neighbour, the mainstay
No ordinary neighbour, this artist, I must say
Requires divine input, to humbly engage
For, no one knows what The Father does !!!
Except, The Son, and vice versa
And whoever they decide really wants
Not a move open to all, no
But few, who desire Heavenly matters, to know
To majority, oblivious, elusive, should emphasise, so
Again, world, to this, is very blind
Will only be available to The Heavenly inclined
World can never acquire, with this climb
Why, world needs waking up, for help
Help, readily available from Heaven in depth
Without Doctor, all, living evil's pandemic death
We have some way to go to get out
But when alerted, we are full of doubt
Thinking, we know what Heaven is all about
No more time, world, to delay
All set, now, with Doctor, Heavenly, portray
For, none cardinal, yet thinking we're okay
With evidence pointing against that
To Heaven, in our faces, we've fallen flat

Shortening proposed eternal span
Goal achievement requires Doctor's turnaround
Who has His feet firmly on the ground?
The One Doctor, in whom we are all sound

RECONCILING WITH HEAVEN THE GOAL
REQUIRES, FORSAKING, COMFORT ZONE
THUS, HEAVENLY GRACE, TO BE WHOLE
ONLY JESUS DOES PROVIDE THIS GRACE
ALPHA, SAVIOUR WHO SHOWS HIS FACE
OMEGA MESSIAH LEADS WINNING RACE
SO, WAKE UP FROM THIS SLEEP, WORLD
PROVE, WITH DEEDS, HAVE, THE THIRST
YES, CLASSED AS HEAVEN'S VERY BEST

CHAPTER TWO

The Doctor

Hence, The Director of Congested Traffic on Roads
The Dealership whose refit eternally holds
Religions, at best, managed to wash, outermost
Yet, this director of congested traffic on roads
Knows escape route for each, back home
Peacefully enjoying family life with all, new and old
Director of congested traffic on roads
Ably shifts trouble-shooting zones
To areas far away from peaceful domes
Director of congested traffic on roads
The one who hasn't lost a single soul
Therefore, to everyone, the defined oath
Using one person to conquer nations
Tiny, disregarded vagabond, with His notion
Ushers David, evil silenced, he motions
Yes, removing life-changing deadly clots
Hurls them, us, steadfast on blocks
Ready for the race, to gain first spot
Curing sins, worse than any cancers

Ensuring our strength, without weakness
Astounding who knew us fading, in these worlds
He shifts congested sins from inside us
Those blocking free, Heavenly breath
To finally, eternally, with Him, rest
Only He dumps without environmental repercussions
No carbon emissions, warranting unsavoury demonstrations
His touch, rather, cleansing atmospheric contaminations

Director Of Congested Traffic On Roads-DOCTOR
The One and Only Messenger, Mentor
JESUS, who speaks for all who need a lecture
The congested road to Heaven's, One Liberator
The one assigned as the Ultimate Orchestrator
His style, rating as the only freedom fighter
Tactics to everyone, everything, out-manoeuvre
State-of-the-art, renowned architecture
Baffling all, without and within the sector
Salvation can only be sorted by This Manufacturer
Sole dealership, fixing into stunning stunner
JESUS, who worthily demonstrates, The Only Saviour
Specially customized cars, made by one, very agile
Each of unique quality, delicate, complex, qualify
Requiring one who identifies each unusual style
Only one person performs these works
Authority of The Son, Messenger, whatever, JESUS
One always among us, yet, world keenly expects
Yes, ultimate goal, to feel Overall Boss
Contouring the lost to become tops
Letting the haughty appear pathetic flops

World juggles around Him, without knowledge
The One Bridge from whom comes the privilege
To attend Heaven's prestigious, eternal College
Not the kind that teaches, living deceit
Evident in our daily deeds, as receipts
Deceitfully, making us think, Heaven is received
Yeshua, Nabi Issa, JESUS, that most await
Some thinking, He has delayed
Chosen One, to eventually save
The one Mediator and Saviour like no other
To yank us from the deep and eminent danger
May we dash into His open arms to live forever
Expecting Him, signals, loss in Heavenly
Clearly, indicating, inept immaturity
Therefore, needing His humble Authority
BLACKSMITH continually hitting requires attention
Repeating self, needs shifting from deadly devotion
Stopping wailing within, to cut evil communication
Said, quoted 25 times in The "Holy Koran"
JESUS, Heavenly messenger of special kind
To come again, of a peculiar clan

Main character in the "Holy Bible"
The Word, providing meaningful cycle
Followed, accordingly, accorded eternal title
In "Holy Tora", His coming, headline news
Simeon, others, wished to witness event too
Eventually, arrived, received by few
Hindus revered Him, holy man, Sadhu
Proud to be associated with the man, Ishu

Embracing Him, warning, more worldly issues
Yeah, JESUS, bigger than any religion
Lifting ALL from fatal dungeons
Beyond Heavenly clad junctions
After each receiving spiritual, physical, truncheons
Pronounced dead after merciless bludgeoning
Only one, who pieces together wholly, as surgeon
Before reaching Him, spotted from distance
Readiness not by mouth, substance
To acquire from Him, real deliverance
Before Him, no slave, no master
No, no Jew or gentile
Ready for who is ready, who-so-ever
Makes, most productive product
Everything priceless, His might conducts
Seeking heart, with Heaven, connects
Beginning, knowing who we, individually, are
Start to understand this marvellous Star
For, the gap between us and Him, very far
He ensures, colours, firmly with Heavenly mast
For, whosoever entering Heaven, a must
Avoiding being cast outside breakwaters, fast
No earthly nations appeal to Him
But, making nations of who adores His vim
Only, daring willing hearts, surely win
This man, amazingly, exclusively, special
Drawing Heaven's attention, earthly residentials
Has some super extra unimaginable credentials
When claiming to be Him, own pastor refused
Because JESUS' spiritual nature, he couldn't deduce

So, into carcass, was he keen to see JESUS reduced
However, Heavenly Baptist, before Him, bowed
JESUS, refused, not wanting a crowd
Demonstrating HUMILITY of distinctive clout!!!

Trusted, traditionally breaking unheavenly traditions
Shattering evil stronghold, with utter conviction
Giving us absolutely revered Heavenly conclusions
Yeah, when Prominent one leaves his residence
With motorcades in precedence
The mission, of extra importance
All accept JESUS, preceded by someone else
A true messenger who really cares
The kind, world, never, truly, caress
We all need The Doctor, JESUS APP
Which does only lift us up
Receiving from Heaven, a healthy clap
One App doing all for all
Knowledge embedded in the slot
No one's qualifications from anywhere, any more
Sole requirement, willing heart
All directions to faithfully follow without fright
Courage to soldier on, day and night
Who wouldn't, seriously, want to boast of it?
Who won't want controls, in this?
Would be amazed to know someone wouldn't
Amazingly, free of charge
That's certainly not a farce
The joy from which we will never part
All evil bailiff worries gone forever

Manipulating figures from taxes, now yonder
Oh, who would want to avoid this, I wonder?
Showing off phones as though, free
Same putting us in trouble, indeed
Hell breaks loose with unpardonable damning deeds
Mobile phones, killing us slowly
Often, destroying knowingly
Would dearly seek JESUS App only
When young, things are revered
While ignorant, advice against them, severe
When mature, realise, should have adhered
So, me too, JESUS, The One-Man Band
To meet in a heartbeat, to wholly understand
Journeying like the apostles, a finish, grandstand
The Only Omnipresent Omniscient Omnipotent One
Sole **G**overnor **O**wner Leader **D**eliverer Bar None
Architect, Beaming Constructive Designs Like No Man
Word, Creator of Heaven and earth
Authority, with Blessed Confirming WORD
Ultimate Overall who was, is, and always in here
If we could accept, we are raw
Surrendering to eternal repentance calls
Instead of relying on filthy prayers and roars
I thank Your tough love to know You more
Continually acknowledging, In You, the best ore
Living manna to let me Heavenly soar
Speaking for all who feel You the same
And who desire to know The Way
Yes, The Way, The Truth, The Life, *everyday*

You do not come for a set outward identity
But for all, this global infirmity
All, open hearts belonging to Your community
Doctor, thanking opportunity bestowed on even me
Shedding some light for re-awakening
Assumed You, but, traveling opposite, indeed
Thank You, for responding, I, call You, Father
No success story, beats this feeling, Master
May I continue holding onto You conducting, farther
World, for the world to be your oyster
Should follow lead of orchestra
Conducted by Original Orchestrator
Yes, Word made tangible, to know and grow
Receiving power from staying in You, to show
Like, stream adhering, into sea, diligently flow
Confirming, Spirit, hence, worship, as such, in truth
Just Eternal Saviour Uniquely Supreme, JESUS, cue
For everything made, through You, by You
I cannot wait to say, JESUS is LORD
As You've declared, a spiritual war
Which, only few win, among all
No, cannot wait to say, JESUS is Lord
For equally, am I sinfully living as born
Not verbal confession, have been warned
Going on about JESUS being Lord
Thinking, speaking favourably about God
Not knowing, He doesn't recognise that call
Stop saying JESUS is Lord!!!
While deeds opposite, an insult
Let us first become very worthy salt

Who wants to say, "JESUS is Lord"?
Let him seek JESUS and ask if it is wrong
To know what is an accepted norm
Exuberant supporters of "JESUS is Lord"
Gladly fashioned in so many forms
Humble hearts, with deeds, calls, receive response
So, arguing about JESUS is Lord, not, pathetic!!!
Showing, spiritually backwards, best, static
Behaving unreasonably, manic
Doctor, forever Master of Change
Demonstrating, just a stage
We, take it, for famed, naive pilgrimage
Slow caterpillar changes into flying butterfly
The Only One with ability, to this, readily apply
For, tiny tries, just cannot justify

Without You, Lord, we always struggle
Without captivation to perfectly juggle
Conversely, only nous, to be in muddle
Spiritual leaders alike, sadly grope
With everything available on the road
Desperate, in achieving devilish goals
No, none truly cuts the mustard
But, calling each other bastard
In our hearts and on placards
So, needing, where, if one says, Shalom
With the heart, within the shire's lawns
Echoing shouts from Heavenly Kingdom
When another dearly says, Peace
Addressee, not portrayed as worthless piece

But, in congruence with Heaven's heartbeat
Equally, when one gratefully portrays Islam
Flowing with deeds that don't slam
But that, which uplifts, even if, from a slum
Should there be, Santi-sandhi
Would depict Heavenly sanity
Breathing through corridors, saintly
Honestly, we haven't grasped own religions!!!
Thus, divisions, unanswered questions
So, no fulfilment in regurgitations
Therefore, needing to learn lessons
To receive Holy One's humble blessings
Before, situation, worsens
Religions haven't provided answers
Clutching on straws, world, Heavenly, staggers
Not intention of true prophets
Confessing, in Holies, not deserved
A place, clean heart, seeking, reserved
Eternity, then, assuredly, preserved
Needing to go back where Adam was
Created, humbly, in image, of AWES
Mind-set, acceptable to The Doctor, Lord
To God's will, on eternal course
In Adam, all smooth, nothing coarse
On same strand of Heavenly resource
Having full understanding of life
Heavenly, natural world, today's wild
Godly, without struggles, knowledge in his stride
So, go back to where you came from
Shouldn't make one feel withdrawn

But stirred up for quality divine romp
So, return to where you came from
Should not cause a frown
But, alive, green, not yellowish-brown

Receiving inner colour of Sacred Crown
Not acquired from pickings from ground
But, hearts rendering, Heavenly turnaround
Yes, to Heaven, enjoying angelic frisks
Where brothers, sisters together pull strings
In humble, graciously entertaining tricks
When message hits you
Opportunity not to miss, to rue
Time to pack up, world, true
Touched by this hint, in honesty
Should seek Heavenly modesty
Propelling journey to Doctor's Majestic Majesty
With Almighty God leading all along
Bonding in oneness where we belong
Absolutely united with The Lord, should throng
Perfectly controlling everything sacred
For, before God, no secret
Acquiring, maintaining this pathway, savoury
Examples from Adam to David, off the charts
Transparency exemplary, according to stats
World needs quick, Heavenly starts
For all are dead alive !!!
Atheists, better, fashioning nothing right
Never touching Heavenly angels, beyond skies
To Doctor, new beginnings

Old self gradually leaves, now, new briefings
Dead air replaced, Heavenly breathings
Should be lucky, having offer again
From Only One who truly reigns
Gifting eternal, successful gains
Prodigal son, realizing, losing shield
Responds to Doctor's call, to shift
Back home, safely, he made it swift
Forever grateful to You, Lord
Emphasising, not verbally pour
But activating Heavenly vigour as norm
One and Only Heavenly Activator
May we continue appreciating Your Indicator
True, Heavenly Motivator
Leading to best of places
Appreciating, cleansing in phases
Graciously, fitting into best of Palaces
You deserve praises, Heavenly *Right*
Preserving, presenting trials
Backing, through Heavenly mires
From birth, we weren't winning
You work hard, freeing us, wilting
Your illustrious desires, for Heavenly weaning

Looking us up, our situations, addressed
Renewing vigour, future, to access
Boldly leading onto path of success
Selecting all backgrounds, religions
Incorporating various regions
Accommodation, avoiding dungeons

Not dwelling on negative rubbish
For exuberant prospects to relinquish
But, instilling verve to accomplish
Dealing with wrong deeds, deceptive
Naturally, not over-looking anything destructive
Managing, onto everything constructive
From poor in spirit, to full steam
Seeking answers without and within
Going out of way, gratifying, dreams
From setbacks, relaunching comebacks
Doing so, we're not aback
Deserving glorious pat on back
You pillar of consolation
Hope, in otherwise, utter devastation
Chance to enjoy Heavenly corporation
Heavenly Doctor, standing bold and tall
Elusive way, providing thick wall
For stakeholders without a fall
You alone, more than enough
From East, West, South, North
Placing us prestigiously, as norm
You are above terrific
Our buzz, fantastically electric
With You, Heavenly eccentric
We continually use predecessors' quotes
While behaviours reduce scope
Diminishing, Heavenly, assumed hope
Passionately confirming brethren quotes
Yet, attitudes, far from Heavenly Throne
So, daily crying, cannot cope

Thinking by quotes
Heading closer home
But rowing sadly into enemy's zone
No healing, quoting "Holy Book" quotes
The Doctor, only one who knows
Prescription required, making all whole
Enlightening about Your environment
Ensures positive mental development
Succeeding in Heavenly compliments
You equip us, managing projects
Optimally prepared as major prospects
Projected top-wise as fast as rockets

Without hope of escaping pit-hole
Your hospitable, healthy leading role
Makes us stronger, whole
Your status, remains on lips forever
Progressing our dreams further
With, and in You, we progress farther
Generations praise Your name
For Your worth, not a game
Acquiring knowledge, we're not same
Hence, eulogised in victory
Murmurs, dangers, to You, history
Literature reviewed, songs, poetry
Sore fingers, now play masterly drums
Medicinal teachings through humble eardrums
Far cry, from days in doldrums
Without alphabet, now, playing piano
Your gift, not punt at bingo

In You, victory, 100% ratio
When trees bear fruit, roots, often forgotten
While working, values are gotten
Doc, Your quality stature never rotten
At height of our darkest hour
Your assurance, never remains sour
We'll reign with You from The Tower
Woes, won't be worse or still
In our favour, would it tilt
With honours at top of the hill
Removing weakness, installed us, champions
Those managing to daily conform
Upholding, called, legendary icons
Thank You, not, by word
For You fill Heaven and earth
Heart-felt actions, show what we share
We appreciate You, Ultimate Sir
Being readily Sacred to dare
Who couldn't care, in awe, they stare
For, like Adam, also naming most things
Would be glad in those leagues
Through us, The Omnipresent, speaks and indeed:

Appreciates awoken, Almighty Air, announced
Baby, beaming bespoke blessings, baptized
Canopy cultures coordinated communication, customized
Defining deeds, designing diverse departments
Embracing everyone everywhere, enjoying environment
Faithfully, feeding famished, feeling fulfilment
Gigantic goodies, glorifying God Graciously

Harmonising highly humorous hymns humbly
Invoking impartial indicators impressively, innocently
Jurisdictions, jointly, justifiably jumping joyfully
Kingdom kindergarten knowledge keyed, kindly
Love leads, loyally, lavishing liberation
Manufacturer's models magnify meekness maturely
Nurturing nonentities, nourishing nostalgia naturally
Omnipotent, orderly orchestrating organisation openly
Patiently, progressively, pre-empting perfect parity
Queueing queens quietly qualifying quality
Remnants, rhythmically rallying righteousness, readily
Saviour's systems, showing salvational seed
Tastefully truthful, Teacher's telepathic tree
Uniquely understanding unequivocally uniformly
Vehemently validating valuable victorious vision
Writing words with worthy wisdom
X-rayed, xeric xenomorphic xylophonic xenia
Yearning youthful yardstick yielding yonder
Zesty Zero, Zooming Zionic, Zenith

SEEK YE DOCTOR FIRST, THE GOAL, TRULY, REAL
IN IDENTIFYING EDITING, EMBRACING, THE DEAL
FOR THE HEAVENLY REALM TRULY FREELY SEAL
AND, YES, WISHED, I WAS TRULY, A CHILD AGAIN
TO CORRECT, TERRIBLE MISTAKES, I, HAVE MADE
NO, WE DO NOT WANT HIM TO, AGAIN, PROCLAIM
AND, OWN RECEIVED HIM NOT, VERY GRUESOME
ONENESS, WITH, THE HEAVENS, WE'LL, BLOSSOM
OH, IN HIM, BECOMING INEXPLICABLY, WINSOME
YES, AWAKE, UP, MYSTERIOUS WORLD, WAKE, UP

CHAPTER THREE

Innocence Tainted

With one voice, we entered world, crying the same
Nine months, all, generally maintained
Carried, naked, onto this place
Always, felt warm
Then, feeling sawn-off, born
Sometimes inexplicably torn
Duly protected, caressed
Needs, timely addressed
Attention-wise, we're first
Enjoying everyone here, brother
Feeling, every girl, sister
Seeing adults, mother, father
We cried, when alone
Bonding, now, no one at home?
Definitely, Not good for the soul
Feeling sleepy, we cried
Telling mummy, we tried
Awake to find, tears dried
We enjoy laughter

All, we're all after
Learning from the master

Playing, crawling, same as a game
Wobbling, falling, holding onto someone, same
Clapping, smiling, taking baby steps, in the main
Growing, stepping out so proud
Surely pulling a crowd
One love, we're allowed
Waving heartily to all
Not caring, who we saw
Always having a ball
The kind, not expensive
Captures all, very impulsive
Oh, so nicely decorative
The ball, genuinely inclusive
To all, openly decisive
But adults, obviously evasive
Enjoying every food
For in our world prevails this mood
Knowing everyone is good
Happy-go-lucky with smiles
Desiring friends, without fright
Living in the land of heights
Landed, in arena of giants
Freedom always, every stride
Looking up to parents, setting our sights !!!
To school, seeing mates
"Let go off me, mum, too slow at this rate"
"Seriously, man, any faster pace?"

We desire each other's company
To us, exact extension of family
As folks, under one canopy
Innocence at its peak
Displayed always, including streets
Enjoying precious, priceless feed
Heartfelt innocence being real
Which is no mean feat
Valuable asset, required to breed
Yes, innocence we cannot demean
Very essential drumbeat
Featuring always, no matter the heat
One innocence, at peak
Demonstrating truth indeed
Never accepted with cold feet
We entered world with innocence
Hopping around in joyous prominence
Mingling with all, oozing confidence
Innocent about race, creed, religion, colour…
To us, non-existent, didn't matter
Just relishing purified laughter

Bad Now Good

Then, inside, something not right
Hot sunny day, frozen, winter night
Open joy, but feeling spiked
Receiving mixed messages
What, now, colleagues, friends, savages?
Where from conflicting images?

Downing smiles, upping frowns
Calculated smiles, frowning crowned !!!
Wickedness increased, laughter, drowned
Do not know who, individually are, anymore
No clue, initially, at all
Although, were happy, now, a new dawn !!!
Never really knew, guess, wrongly thought
Where are we, now, just not the norm
What is strangely happening, must be a storm
Beginnings of asking questions
Out of regular fashion
To whom, can we, this mention?
Snowballing, brains going fuzzy
Entire body, now feeling funny
Oh no, feeling dizzy
Mummy, daddy, we tried
All adults, same replied
Left with own devices, we cry
Sailing against the tide
Who has strength to be on our side
Only Heaven avoids capsize
Rowing against the waves
Greatest obstacle, we've come against
Only Heaven, to our aid !!!
Chopping iron with hands, dare not bite!!!
Who has this chisel's might
Only Heaven cuts, into orderly file!!!
Into sinful world, slowly merged
Anger, hatred, ignorance, gradually surged
Goodwill, wiped off, submerged

Innocent classmates, now enemies
Sinful sickness, overtaken goodies !!!
Talking good, feeding from hades
Parents, adults, peers' teachings?
With what, were they feeding?
Tainted innocence, badly seething
Brothers, sisters, viciously divided
Innocent innocence, dangerously subsided
Oneness, no longer divinely resided

Colour, ethnicity intensified, no more smiles
Greed, selfishness, anger, improves downward slides
Society, now, dealing with plight
Community, burying, nursing, victims of crimes
Who caused these internal grimes?
Genuine understanding, no longer rhymes
To a halt, it now grinds
Society dealing with victims of crime
Mummies, inconsolable in their cries
Good dynamics, supplanted with bad
All living, at best, very sad
Innocent, now destroying like mad
Community searching for its soul
Dumped, deeply into abysmal hole
Who, to even identify it, to know?
Growing up brothers, neighbours
Now, fully grown strangers
Who caused hatred among us?
No… own brothers, now, I so much hate
What happened to one human race?

Knowing, all, truly born, same
How… loved ones, now, I so much distaste?
What happened to all those lovely dates?
Why… have I, now, been replaced?
What is the basis, I very much hate?
Yet, reunions were not fake
So, why, intense hate traits?
Why, so much nepotism?
Where from antisemitism?
Oh, why burning with anti-Islamism?
Why so much racism?
Unrelenting tribalism?
Goodness, so much pessimism
There is blackness in whitism
As much as whiteness in blackism
If only we could wise up and reason
Should arrive at it, even if, called names
Demonstrating positive traits
With absolute humility, now, and future age
Should be expected, embraced mantra
Opportunity, replicating The Master
For others to appreciate, The One Father
When we truly know who we, each, are
Would enjoy these moments, better
Showing how we've climbed some strata
Heavenly co-ordinated social responsibility
Would be abused, denied, welcoming hospitality
Yes, time to tell, above negative publicity

Demonstrating, when one right, other wrong

In fact, both wrong, according to Heavenly norms
For, all sinful, hence, needing Heavenly reform
Showing that when one wrong, the other right
Accredited right has no right to strike
But realising, I am, my brother
Letting go, moving on, breeds mature oneness
Accepted on earth and Heaven with gladness
Triggering, new mature trend, loving kindness
Cutting out unwanted bad climate
Making everyone suffocate
Up to our necks, decisions, eventually make
Only if we knew there is blackness in white
A definite whiteness in black
Would save lives with oneness, without fights
If we just knew we're brothers, as one
Loving the union, definitely not bland
Will know, this, definitely not a bluff
If we know how evil teases about racism
Worsened, by killing, for tribalism
Sad world, destroys for chauvinism
Epitome of depth in lost jungle
But, truthfully, one same people
We are shamefully, deluded bundle
Living, horrible life of delusion
Regifting evil, Heavenly, for misconception
Pathetically destroying each for deception
Wasting time fighting, killing, about lies
Forgetting, one day, we'll all die
Oh, when will we start having close ties?
When racism, tribalism, won't come to mind

Ah, evil rejoicing, for our minds, able to wind
Taken control of real human spine
If we knew religion is one
Doing what The Heavenly Father wants
We wander under evil wand
Running same race with pandemonium
Ruling with fist more potent than abused opium
Not realizing, under magical spell, conundrum
Should quickly seek Heavenly restitution
To live joyfully, as people under renovation
Inwardly, outwardly, truly, founded restoration
Should remember, body requiring redecoration
Befitting temple of God needing rehabilitation
For The Omnipotent to admire, a re-installation
Designed by The Greatest Artist alive
Sculptured for us to appreciate Him, wise
The Potter's handywork moulded to excite

Rather, the basis for devastating precipice
We, and our ignorance, thus, never known peace
Crown jewels shattered yet feeling appeased
Thinking we know, but living in ignorant ignorance
For, no Heavenly concordance
To culture, cemented, cohesive song and dance
Thinking we don't need anyone's help
Because, can do it ourselves
Dangerous, needing very good steps
Yes, but in truth, who wasn't?
Who has not prayed for help, who hasn't?
Who does not call for help, who doesn't?

Reason why we need revamping
To suit right stance, a rebuilding
A makeover, thorough re-conditioning
Should all drop stinking egos !!!
Realizing, Heaven, only one option goes
Desire to grow whole !!!
So, should drop nasty egos
Like wasted rotten mangoes
Definitely not like enjoying banjos
We are all full of faults
But something we can halt
Starting, giving foolish pride a jolt
Toddlers, never kept apart
Doing all, with pure hearts
Borne out of innocent parts
Never thought would fall apart
Making complicated life, simple work of art
How many "educated" adults really play this part?
Living humbly like ones we call kids
Showing innocent kindness as off-springs?
Who genuinely behave as the striplings?
.We fully teach youth envy
Their burdens we then pay as sinful levy
How do we get out each, to all, around, rally?
We were genuinely inseparable
Oozing oneness, always adjustable
As brothers and sisters, dearly compatible
Oh, when will those days come again?
Those days, absolute bargains !!!
We easily call those times, Haven !!!

We don't appreciate value, till lost
With free living at cheapest cost
Reflecting, undoubtedly, at a loss
Physically, mentally, financially, especially, spiritually
We lost all joy from purity very quickly !!!
Assumed knowledgeable, used assets foolishly

We are what we think
We could think it, a jinx
Or floating with gracious mix
You are precisely what you think
On the path of Holy Indelible ink
Or deceived into ever evaporating mint
Yes, we are what we think
Causing us to deeply sink
Or make it big, with eyes, blinked
Being who and how we think
We could assume it, a myth
Or flowing with a gracious fix
Yes, we are what we think
On Holy Indelible ink things
Or enjoying cosy fur of mink
Deception, including, refusal to admit errors
Perfectionists without substance, cause tumult
To garner respect, better than lying, for uproar
Why smashing rackets on floors?
Disappointed with scores?
Who plans where to hit ball?
No one wants being at fault
Yet, no one, Heavenly, has good thoughts

For, we daily plan evil plots
None admits guilt, to be at fault
Yet, Heavenly deeds, we always dodge
For, Heavenly angels we badly fought
Pointing fingers to others as at fault
Yet, to evil, are we all betrothed
What good can we really conjure?
When smashing rackets on floors
They don't direct course
Always at our mercy on all fours!!!
Pointing finger at another at fault
Rest pointing more
Directly to pointer's amiable evil font
Never want to be associated with faults
Yet, in line with human natural folklore
Evil comes out of us with powerful volts
Why smashing rackets on floors ?
When not architect of our fall?
Considering, result of own flaws !!!
Nonsense, smashing rackets on floors
Does not call scores!!!
But then, whose fault?
Cease smashing rackets on floors
They cannot be the cause
Not cause of flaws, own downfalls!!!

Bad results, smashing rackets on floors
When helping to stand tall
Failures create gripping laws !!!
Humans seek others to blame

Instead of self to plane
To avoid indefinite wane
Not me, his, hers, their fault
Constant response, put forth
Yet, no good, have we sought
Appearances are sometimes deceptive !!!
Beware, Messiah comes a thief !!!
Be, therefore, astute spiritual detective
All smash rackets in different ways
Refusing tasks Heaven anticipates
To teaming up with forlorn soulmates
We continually point anger to others
When own egos blaze unwanted tempers
Heaven smiles, fanning with cool feathers
Who claims to have no fault?
Does the person want to be pillar of salt?
For sin is just like evil, earthly cult
Bad becomes good in worldly eyes
Requiring changes in lifestyles
To stop the deadly landslides
Abominations are warmly embraced
Enticing all to join the race
Quickly grabbing like a craze
Bad, norm of day
Oh, would get away with it, it's okay
Anything, acceptable in the way
Abominations are writhe, being hay
Nothing about being gay
Enough dirt, called decay
Bad a pandemic, okay to groom

Growing trend for mellow moods
Not confined to the hood
From cheer leaders to children
Legalised, so chill then
Mandatory ritual hence
Pandemic, bad, no panic
Innovating, can't stay static
To be best, be drastic

When bad becomes good
And abominations, embraced
Who foretells the next stage?
With bad, now, accepted, sane
And abominable cravings, as sage
Who'll be left, to anyone save?
Everyone, sinner, completely tipped over
Desires for own justices, never sober
Dangerously, choosing, seconds, toner
None fears one, called God
From prim and proper to worldly off course
Can time it, without being caught
Other, partner, cannot see, so, okay
Yet, good morning, good day, we always say
No good in us, to make goodness stay
Peace, shalom, as salaam alaikum, brother
Fooling selves, daily, in this manner
Refusing to Heavenly, surrender
When are we, to be awake?
In anguish can we only gape
For, Heavenly anger, we cannot escape

WHY HAS THE GOOD DREAM LIFESTYLE CEASED?
WHEN WILL ALL IDENTIFY, EMBRACE THIS, REAL?
BAD BECOMING GOOD, WHEN HEAVEN TO SEAL?
NOW WISHED WOULDN'T SMASH RACKETS AGAIN
TO CORRECT, GRAVELY MISTAKES, HEAVEN SAKE
YES ENSURE THERE'S NO VOID IN HEART'S PLACE
FATAL VOID MAKES EVERY SITUATION WOESOME
TRULY, HEAVENLY ONENESS MAKES US BLOSSOM
IN OUR AWE BECOMING INEXPLICABLY WINSOME
THUS, LET US AWAKE, ALL, WAKE UP, OH WORLD!!!

CHAPTER FOUR

Wake Up, Oh World

So, awake, people awake
Let's try, to something, change
To avoid massive impending carnage
Rejuvenate, Heavenly, oh world
Though late, Heaven, ready to mend
Another day, and none able to weld
Wake up, wake up, deadly dead
For all that twirled
Soon, to be hurled
Stimulate lovingly, oh world
This isn't first, second or third
Complexities, Heaven has upheld
So, try, wake up, oh world
For all, at whom you snarled
Seeing how you, and enemy has gelled
Liven up, miserable worldly expert
Your type has been seen and heard
In the end, they all yelled
Revitalize, world, be shaken with fear

Forget thoughts, held, and cared
For stomachs, soon will be curled

Quicken stance out of here
This cry to you, may sound weird
But lava, rushing to beard
Be aroused out of this dearth
Your ministers, living cursed
Who then, will not be felled?
Hence, please, be motivated world
When your milk will no longer curd
Then you know, Heaven no longer cares
Get out of this worldly mess
As the gigs become tears
The Heavenly will then be yearned?
So, wake up, from scantiness
You that whispered and fish heard
Won't command your beard when you yell
Dare, therefore, change, world
Handsome giant pulling every girl
Before death, to you, becomes a pearl
Casting mind back, world
After joyous birth
You couldn't say a word
Remember those days, world
When, very vulnerable, yet well fed
You, innocent loving pet
Revisit those times then, world
How ill, you, at times were
All hoped, you'll be well

Stronger, physically, now, world
But should also beware
Divinely, haven't improved from scarceness
Truthfully, world, you've retrogressed
Of all set plans, been goalless
Taking short-cuts, you're homeless
All prompts, remaining undeterred
Worldly lunacy, continually preferred
Hence, Heaven's, decision, you're referred
Brethren in "Holy books", deserted world
Addressing them, putting cautions to bed
Their names, Heaven indelibly pen
Miserable ways, ringing loudly like a bell
From distance, aroma, Heaven can tell
What is there to sell?
Causing so much nuisance
Near and afar-off distance
Time to admit, just a pittance !!!
Trauma listings, endless
Leaving us Heavenly penniless
The only saviour, Heavenly Wonders!!!

"Holy Book" brethren, followed what was said
For, bodies, minds, soul, Heavenly, was set
So, dreaded beasts, away, were they swept
To worthlessness, have we been dedicated
Thinking everyone, we have manipulated
Death sentence, being adjudicated
Behaviours cause major storms
Which should not be the norm

Ignorance hardens, getting back to form !!
Worldly behaviour, sets us rocking
Getting everyone concerned and talking
While doors, Heaven, consistently knocking
We've caused damaging uproar
Written on Heavenly corridors
Insane, thinking, avoiding enemy's paws
When young, looked so fine
Renowned heir, duly in line
Oh, if we could dearly, reverse time
While young, spoke right words
Climbing up right stairs
Duly attending right fairs
Speaking so softly
Behaving so much humbly
Doing everything rightly, promptly
On Heavenly thoroughfare
A clean heart, that was bare
What happened, for all now, we, to stare?
Were on Heavenly thoroughfare
To everyone, very fair
What changed, world, for such a stir?
Wake up, therefore, from sparseness
Cards are stacked against us
Alas, poor Yorick, henpecked!!!
With albatross around one's neck
Boastings, to Heaven, overly swelled
Into the abyss, soon, be swirled
Noticing fresh buckets of sweat
Our days, surely numbered

Should seek Healer, after all others
Who wants to join The Maestro?
Should demonstrate virtuoso
To be in congruence with The Supremo
This stage, wheels cannot move slowly
Should be fast to become homely
Hastening, to join the wholly
Should be extra humbly radical
At this level, very pivotal
Before, into the dead, we're spiralled

All we do, put the cart before the horse
Yet, Heavenly, we say we are on course
On evil course our definite source
Always done things the wrong way
But will not zip up, from going astray
Knowing Heaven renders best pay
Continually shoving off corrective measures
Diving into destructive waters
What have we achieved, sad pretenders?

Iron Fist in Velvet Glove

World, do not underestimate The lord
Epitome of iron fist in velvet glove
Very kind, yet unparalleled wrath
Be, not fooled, by The Lord
Decorated symbol of warmth
Change idea; do anything, pray, its gone
Wrong to disregard iron fist in velvet glove

For, in all things, has the final call
Like Job, He, called the shots
Should deal with Him, trembling
Cannot be fooled, good, resembling
Upgrade therefore for Heavenly, trending
When The Lord cited His Prayer
Never about His Word to utter
But, living the prayer, Heavenly, better
Prayer, supposed guiding light
Leading happily in Heavenly spotlight
For joyful reunion in serene candlelight
Illuminating, like brilliance of skylight
Showing rays of light, from each lifestyle
Therefore, not needing anyone's light
So, Heavenly Father, hallowed be His name
When identified, His will, displayed
The Kingdom come, living The Way
His will, not being done as in Heaven
Need repentance, brethren
Seeing pathetic lives, we're living
From this, can we never divert?
This reminder, for better, cannot digress
Away from Heavenly directives, current distress
The daily bread, not worldly food
Not money, either, been fooled
So, reciting, does not equate good

None shows green shoots of recovery
Not even slim pickings
Who desires being masterly, speedy?

No one even tiptoes
To be accredited, a go slow
Asleep world, in evil, heavily soaked
Should urge, for sacred platform
Needing wake-up call, for the podium
Strong run, for the rostrum
Torrential currents, strongly gathering
At blistering pace, fast approaching
How does crippled world avoid this closing-in?
Talking good, living opposite
Tearing into others, supposedly, don't think
Yet, supposed thinkers' behaviours really stink
Hence, with all supposed good intentions
Breathe out hot air, of devastation
Fire, destroying continuous generations
Heaven, fed up with words without works
So very disrespectful, it hurts
Portraying depth of unpardonable curse
The bread, His Daily Fresh Word
To guide, straighten our every curve
The evil one's company to equally swerve
Yes, one that can only be frenetic
All the devotion to ensure it is emphatic
Here, it can never be empathetic
Each, concentrating on tasks, enthralling
With all tools, making it, engrossing
All eyes fixed on you, very indulging
Yes, we accept, The Heavens, our Holy Grail
Accepting also, hades, not a lonely grave
Therefore, destined, sadly, for sinful slave

Every mountain, climbable, should we dare
Should remember, not from this earth
Because God, truthfully, no human serves
For, not being equipped enough, in frailty
Needing strength to overcome jeopardy
From same "Heaven", who overcomes evil strategy?
But who really is the devil?
Including me, every human is evil
Not easy to distil this refill!!
Yes, we've all been extremely monstrous
To our fellow humans, unreasonably callous
In devil's den, very skilfully ambidextrous
We keep saying "the devil is a liar"
"WUOW", we are the devil, making lives dire!!!
Reason, for burning in this fire

Angels who come and go to Heaven
Like one taking steps in, what is, a kitchen
Is what we all seek, haven
Why there is none better than This Master
JESUS who said "come unto me all ye that labour"
Going for help, should be a small matter
Won't wait till little left
When suffering, Saviour takes pain, instead
Just the effort, then, treated as best
The prodigal son did the same
A party, thrown in his name
After having tortured in vain
Heaven does not do time zones
Who wants to avoid ensuing tornadoes?

Soon, eruption of volcanoes
Snow too, will fall, all to freeze
Without any fine daytime breeze
Let all hearken, for, soon, none to breathe
No one, able to survive
Reason why, all should revive
And into The Heavenly mind, seriously drive
For, we're too full of selfishness
Even worse, nasty callousness
Very consumed in hateful wickedness
To evil, so easily magnetic
Behaving so shamelessly, pathetic
Where are, religious mavericks?
Who is prepared to put himself in spotlight?
Anyone for screening when The Candle lights?
For Heaven to recommend, yes, a highlight!!!
We're all, bunch full of destitution
No one moving into restitution
Milking in our lifeless style of convolution
None near being apologetic
Despite feeling something going down, titanic
When the penny drops, can only be manic
Who think Heavenly, they are heroes?
To realize they are not even minnows
For, they are, their own foes
What do we call legacy?
Is it so-called over-hyped charity?
Or, evidently distorted Heavenly mentality?
Heavenly knowledge, nowhere near scintillating
Like children in front of cameras, jubilating

Just because, all can see us loving misbehaving
Heavenly torchlight cannot trace any sunshine
This is our greatest achievement, our paradigm
Despite Heaven calling for bragging rights

Because all are pathetic creeps
Enjoying pleasing the world while we sneak
Out into the wilderness at tremendous speed
It's truly, now or never for a decider
Pre-occupied Martha, lucky to be told the matter
From The Ultimate Overall Messiah Master
Again, we're like Saul before Paul, at best
To Heaven, behaving as nuisance pests
Yet, unarmed at war, no bullet-proof vest
The Heavenly call, world, should not resist
For, consequence thereon, will revisit
From these unscrupulous acts, should desist
Yes, our lifestyles, unworthily destitute
Nothing precious to produce
For Heaven to eagerly nominate, to recruit
What do we have for our offspring?
What are we leaving behind, we, and siblings?
Even now, are we exposed, exemplary families
We thought we had greatest knowledge
Each religion clamouring for the greatest coverage
But, achievement, discovery, unworthy footage
Why we need to cut out ignorant views
To obtain contemporary Heavenly news
And conduct what helps, in reviews
Starting, vehemently, with exuberant youth

Even though, pathetic situation, we cannot refute
Yes, devil's den, can refuse
Beginning with wayward youth
Constantly shying away from books
But, seriously requiring trending goods
Working on untouchable youth
Who assume have all good looks
Strolling into famous headline news
Should be able to educate young
To mind manners, including the tongue
Stopping, I am young, don't count
Who, again, worldly maestros is interested?
Who, to The Heavenly, wishes to be riveted?
How many, into Heavenly streets are captivated?
He is the one JESUS, the only Universal Liberator
The Holy One in whom we don't need verbal prayer
Available for each, to Heavenly prosper
One, oozing brightest brilliance
Shiniest light of unbelievable fluorescence
Yes, with unrivalled magnificence
Brilliance, naked eyes don't appreciate appearance
True gem of brilliance
Overly displaying plumes of fluorescence

Lucky, having unique mediator
Extending reconciliatory arm asunder
Reaching Him, without slightest bother
Needing, breaching gap between us and Heaven
Ensuring, lifestyles, closer to Heavenly brethren
Growing spiritually, actions, bettering

Heavenly paucity, requires waking up, world
When everything no longer, us, will serve
A drop of water, we'll wish to share
Familiarity breeding contempt
"Finders keepers, losers weepers?"
While flattery, gets us nowhere
Find Saviour, world, for keeps
This, no mere preaching, or cooked-up dream
Let's wake up, grab what this means
All too familiar, with various religions
Having, at this point, already made decisions
Not to change, for fear, confusion
Yet, same, was with apostles of old
When message hit home, they left homes
Leaving all, for, eureka, true trove!!!
Never a shame, feeling bemused
Or criminal, being confused
Home has been fatal disputes
No, not strange to question this
Born with void, has damaging consequences
Hollow within, control influences?
Rather a good sign, should we panic
Without which, we're totally manic
Not what Heaven wants, from the summit
So, feeling message in bones
Heavenly re-awakening over vague hope
Grab as much as possible, in vogue
Nothing, no one compares to this opportunity
Awake, seriously, without hanky-panky
From this precarious situation for immortality

Where are the philanthropists?
Who fits in, as true Heavenly activist?
Where are, craftsmen with that blueprint?
Who is the super mega filthy rich?
Philanthropy of Heaven, eternal gift
No kind of gift, truly, would ever reach
The breath we breathe alone, a start
Without which, there is no life
So, whose riches, make telling mark?
Who is the missionary?
Who is confirmed, visionary?
Who, first, being revolutionary?

Wake-up call comes with serious tone
Therefore, certainly, not classic joke
Telling reality, maybe, from a rogue
A nonentity wishing to Heavenly grow
Assuredly not time to say no
Nor time, to go slow
Time, to The Heavenly throne, accede
For, owner, wills all, to succeed
Pivotal, as this world evaporates at speed
Heaven, already in us, to trigger
Only He, does it, with a swagger
The Only One without wither
When do we awake, saying, no more drama
Who, with chink in armour?
Prepared for Heaven's journey planner?
Wake up sensibly, sad press
None demonstrating Heavenly verve

Endeavour to the wickedness, depress
Because, all operations, for earthly dirt
Not about group's word
So, how to The Heavens, is each wed?
Enough of the slumber, world
Losing all that was said
Now on carcass, are we fed
Hope to shape up secular interests
For all, who at us, purred
Would be running helter-skelter, scared
Should know something is wrong, world
When, every grip, is shattered
Crowning glory among others, shared
What have we left, human experts?
With what do we continuously boast then?
When the belled cat, away from us, has fled
What is left then, of meagreness?
When all senses facing a wear
Away from us, to eventually tear
Wherefore, then, them, will we buy, world?
Considering, not even possessing a purse
For, last dime, into the deepest, fell
Facing momentous drill, the worst
No water left in wells
Hence, best friend, unquenchable thirst
Wherefore, thy waters, world?
When we filled up every well
No food, escape, nothing is well
So, pull together, dread

Left naked, nothing to wear
Soon, body fed to worms

Saver what is left under threat
Floor napkins, will no one sell
To know how world, really fared
Where, now heading, world?
From pinnacle to lowest ebb
Fitting, then, into the earth?
Pull together, in dearth
The dead will awake from the earth
With us, nowhere to turn
So, why still asleep, world
To whom are we so wired
Would've thought, we'd be tired
Yet, still, clinging, onto dead
Knowing he hasn't a breath
Cannot even hear a word
Disentangle from this web
Oblivious to hurricane's net
Devastation, chaotic snare
Who claims being "compos mentis?"
Telling Heaven, he really means this
So, getting out of devil's wish-list
Heaven desires attitudes even-tempered
A person, appropriately, down-to-earth
Who is that Heavenly level-headed?
Surely, something seriously amiss
With all the pandemonium in our midst
To still be responding to the snake's hiss

What happened to this world?
Many atrocities, we never fell
Now, can't be identified even among elves
Where are we heading to, world?
Previously controlling all trends?
Where now, are the friends?
Now then, with crazy failures of rareness
Able to mime shouts at best
Sadly bloody tears, our cuddly fest
Therefore, are we distraught
Like, fish in net, are we caught
Final destination, in our hands, not
But, here we are, on spending splurge
The evil kind, putting us on edge
So, even softly speeches, our ears hurt
Heaven, eagerly awaiting
To get closer to the angels, Heavenly
Us, spending time on eternity
For, all before JESUS, simply, inadequate
Hence, in our seats, should we quake
For inability, reaching Heavenly state

Before JESUS, was Nicodemus
Religious head, worldly famous
Sneaking out to JESUS, no Heavenly focus
Nicodemus ordaining many pastors
Everyone obeying these leaders
Their blessings, every follower treasures
Who was to know before JESUS came?
No one questioning Nicodemus claims!!!

Who, even, with nous, to that move, make?
Best thing that ever happened!!!
Imagine, now, hearts, he has saddened
Straying, who, onto him, were fastened
WUOW, for our befallen fate all these years
Sending reinforcements from the devil, us to tear
Therefore, Heaven compassionately sensing fears
We, who evidently operate against the grain
Hoping for what we hope to gain
Without Heaven, none achieving aims
We are all to blame
All being the same
This, not a happy-ending fame
Even competition among siblings from youth
So unbelievable, it is uncouth
But, sadly, that's the truth
Wake up, before so-called paradise is lost !!!
Then, hard work gone with cost
Nothing compared to impending loss
Wake up, for so-called paradise, tossed
Stolen names, in holy holocaust
For none, actually, fits the course
Individuals need own identities
To understand previous and current spirituality
Imagine visiting national president without identity
Each should possess a Heavenly credibility
To such, allotted responsibility
Imagine before the president with stolen ID
Each should obtain own identity
Can't use another's for accountability

Attempting, boarding a plane without ID
No one should plough lonely furrow
Because our ways, not good to follow
Nothing good into bellies, we swallow
Hence, so much rubbish from us, come out
Sins and shortfalls, cannot count
Showing that in spiritually, we are not stout
Anomaly hanging on hanger
Because, about to evaporate yonder
Who runs for cover?

Most sacred of life on earth
Conducted by Mr. Air
Who knows, He could soon be here !!!
Most important part of living
Sustainability by Heaven !!!
Which most think, are having
So, move world, don't stand and stare
Heaven won't wait overly, for years
Ready for those who clearly yearn

Fiasco

Who wants to avoid fiasco?
Who cuts Heavenly gusto?
Avoiding impending dreadful scenario
Who attempts raising crescendo?
As a team, let's not stutter on staccato
But, swing, enjoying, legato
Let none of us be in limbo

But flow with the occasional tremolo
And condescending vibrato
Get out of disastrous ghetto
Yes, out, showing Heavenly bravado
To receive the real eternal gold
By mouth, wanting out of fiasco
Yet, loving evil's intimate fandango
Despite all Heavenly embargo
Who wants to escape this inuendo?
Not time for jolly hello
From The Heavens, get a hullo
Let's avoid intended fiasco
From riverbanks, chaos would overflow
Till, unto Heavenly Road, deeds begin to show
Needing to re-strategize out of this inferno
No lie detector required, attempt to forgo
Reading each DNA logo
Saying, we're ready to skip this fiasco
Changing this long unyielding motto
Yet, worldly allures, continually follow
Who prepares to break away from evil ranks?
And from sin, empty tanks
Displaying to Heaven, been a punk
Who is ready to break ranks?
Call for change, not a prank
Not restricted to obvious drunks

Heaven calls out, to defy evil ranks
Saying, evil, seriously, no thanks
Won't be wasted on riverbank

Who drops coordinated, messy ranks?
Diverting into sustainable eternal tanks
To be divine, sin, eventually sunk
Who desires showing, evil, lowly ranked?
Does deserve among Heavenly monks
Nowhere, no longer near my bunk
Who wishes to avoid this sad momento?
Let him, traditions, disown with gusto
With The Heavens, notable and co
If ready to outgrow this fiasco
Let us, all the nonsense, let go
Latching onto Heavenly lasso
Why still obstinate, world?
Others, this hurdle didn't reach and fell
Yet, ignoring all designs we've felt
To avoid this intended fiasco
Heaven sent angels, helping us know
But, avoided them for worthless egos
Heavenly angels arrive, to all, Heavenly steer
But, we treat them with a sneer
Remaining, therefore, in the rear!!!
Hence, Heavenly anger, always stoked
Because, eye of chosen, we've poked
Consequently, receiving more than brutal shove

WE, CAN MAKE LIFE ETERNITY, SURE REALITY
WHEN SEEKING, LORD'S HEAVENLY SERENITY
REALIZING, THERE IS, NO GRACIOUS INFINITY
THUS, WISHED I WAS RE-BORN A CHILD AGAIN
AVOIDING FIASCO, FROM ERRORS EACH MADE

ENSURING, THERE IS, NO VOID, IN THIS PLACE
ESCAPING, TRUE IRON FIST IN VELVET GLOVE
OH, WITH HEAVENLY ONENESS, YES, BLOSSOM
AND, IN HIM, SURELY, GRACIOUSLY, AWESOME
LET US AWAKE UP, WAKE UP, ALL, OH WORLD!!!

The Jew, claims, he is Heaven's favourite, first
Black man saying, he is Heaven's physical best
White man, maintaining that Supremacy quest
Consequently, no peace, in our lives, with these
Mentioning, additionally, Religious, misgivings
Evidently, causing insane world a few misdeeds
Everyone showing love, buries hatchet and fast
That is what Heaven expects, only quality casts
Gloriously, then, paraded before His elite mass

CHAPTER FIVE

From Adam

Adam starts, Heaven the groom
Ensuring Adam in groove
Dear Adam, King of Eden Group
Adam and The Lord, in tune
Every step a Heavenly move
Accordingly, in Heavenly orchestral mood
Nothing to anyone, prove
Everything, conveniently, swoop !!!
Nothing, no one, to ponder, dupe
Humble Adam in full control
Epitomizing Heavenly scroll
Expressing harmony assured, on a roll
For, Heaven has made him whole
Completely oblivious to hope
Enjoying life in this his home
Adam, not needing blessing
In line, automatic redressing
Daily, life, truly refreshing
When Heaven spoke, in unison

Accepted with purposeful reasoning
Day in day out, all seasons

Human life, then, Godly
Everything said, done normally
With animals peacefully, gorgeously
The Alpha Deity Almighty Made
In him, nothing fake
Didn't need prayers, for anything sake
His faith, joy, devotion, The Lord
With whom he had constant dialogue
Keeping him abreast, rightly informed
Then, alas, noticing, animals, in twos
Observing closely what they do
Thought, had to be him, too
Thoughtfully, seeing animals in twos
Admiring how they woo
Put Adam in some mood
Why not me too, he ponders, Papa?
Me and another, each to pamper
"Good for the goose, good for the gander"
Adam deliberates for a while…
Changing mood, with reducing smiles
The Lord, he should ask why
Thinking of it for a long while
Changing royal lifestyle
Thought it was now time
Hence, from his post, was he drifting
To the unknown, was he shifting
Against The Lord, now, was he living

Oh dear !!!, Adam questions authority !!!
In haughtiness, continues naughty
With time, fades Heavenly Glory
His glory gone, before Eve formed
Eve, replacing Ultimate Lord
Matter of time, for exit door
Adam, now, sweating to eat
Eve suffering before she feeds
Where's the blessing in this feat?
When everything was at Adam's feet
Didn't sweat, no ends to meet
Where's the blessing in this defeat?
When he had every authority!!!
Now, not worth a nonentity
Where, the blessed integrity?
Oh, wake up world!!!
How he wished it could be reversed
Now hating how he felt
Still, had so much, in honesty
But, knew, was in jeopardy–
In bunkers today, thinking, "lovely jubbly"!!!

Expert Advice

When The Heavens announce a curse
Who says it can be worse?
Let him challenge, I fear the worst
Heaven pronounced this life a curse
Yet, we think having money, is best
Boasting in what is Heaven's evil stead

We lust in what Heaven despises
And dislike, good, Heaven advises
Who revels in Heavenly practices?
Whoever, we're descendants of evil
Pointing fingers at others, all, are the devil
Operating, at different levels
Who is first, practising prostitution?
According to Heavenly Institution?
In His Eternal Constitution?
So, who acknowledges Heaven?
I ask the "straight" among the brethren
Who, with The Heavenly bread unleavened?
Who does what Heaven wants?
We, and what our religion chants?
Loving worldly song and dance
Our lives, never up to expectations
Why, with The Lord's, are confrontations
Including me, none key in holy consultations

For, all I say to Him are lies
He reads it all, from my files
And in my fright, He just smiles
All I tell Him daily is rotten
The decay, to Him, yeah, forgotten
In my head, I'm begotten
Yes, begotten because He said so
Not for works, for I would be towed
To hades, the only place I would go
Yes, begotten because He said so
To oblivion, would've been my poor soul

One of many, won't be sole
But He says no, He gladly atones for me,
Who kicks the slash in His knee
Yet, works for me to have eternal glee
He would work to save my life
No matter the pace of my slide
For my sake He would daily try

Who knows this daily Heavenly theme?
A must for all as part of the team
To really enjoy the Heavenly gleam
The Heavenly destination, not assumed
A trail in which daily we are consumed
Especially, when others thinking, confused
Apostles endured this agony
Left homes, all, without a penny
Heavenly trail, never funny
The Heavenly walk, not about black or white
One, we either way, so much spite
We must change for Heavenly respite
Breaking confined boundaries
Never like, others, leaving own countries
Settling, dwelling in new territories
The Heavenly feel, not for the elite
Definitely not for the pauper in need
Only the success through HEAVENLY deed
The Heavenly journey, no dual identity
In Him, or no nationality
Compliance, demonstrating, uniformity
Yes, totally different from norm

Do what we think, get home, be warm?
Goes beyond that, surely, should warn
My Heavenly Father knows, thank You, JESUS
Thank You, Gracious Messenger for lectures
Even though I go back to the vultures
You continually stayed at my door
Lying down for me, as mat, on floor
So, I appeal to Heaven as expected ore
You cleansed soles of apostles' feet of every dust
So, into hades, will not be thrust
Making it into Heaven, even if, only just
You've continually fed me, with your word
Putting back in, though I habitually reject
For my salvation, you've not deterred
To my actions, you've been oblivious
Route to death would've been ominous
For your sake, did not receive the obvious
You left your glory for humanity sake
We of all spoils, to change our fate
What good is in human to deserve this stage?
Yet, You've accredited us with strength
The kind that has unbelievable breadths
Under immeasurable expansive lengths
Telling us, we're planted in your tree
You and your Father in us to be
Just as you first created Eden
Making us the eternal obedient Adam
Your likeness, eternally saying, Abba
Rest of alphabet we await, saying, Amen, Father
This is what we should all aspire to be

These, in "Way of Life", for Him to see
Even before we go down on knees
Oh how great it would be!!!
To have The Father acknowledging indeed
That yes, we've qualified, with good deeds
That would be a wonderful day!!!
To have Him gladly say
You are whole, out of clay!!!

REQUIRING THIS TRUE CHANGE IN MOOD
AS BORN AGAIN, IN REAL, SINCERE TRUTH
SACRED, EXPERT ADVICE, TO BE SMOOTH
YES, WE COULD TRANSFORM INTO BABIES
FREELY ADVERTISING OUR BABY NAPPIES
INHERENT SIN, GONE, FROM OUR PLACES
DISPLACING VOID FOR WHOLESOMENESS
ENJOYING SURREAL HEAVENLY ONENESS
IN HIM, BECOMING RENOWNED WINNERS
ARISE, AWAKE, UP, WAKE UP, ALL. WORLD

CHAPTER SIX

Arise World Arise from Malaise

For the world is descending a steep slope
Who knows the depth and its scope?
Even faster than slalom in the snow
While the world descends a steep slope
No one stops or makes it slow
Everyone, in this disaster, flows
The world doesn't enjoy the slope
For, it hasn't put up a good show
Vultures, waiting, ready to crow
Who stops the unyielding slide?
When topmost receive unrelenting strikes
No one stops disaster in its stride
From the womb to the tomb
There is worldly expected boom
Yet, only one beyond the moon, zooms
From the womb to the moon
There is unworthy expected boom
Yet, only one zooms beyond the tomb

From the tomb, arisen, assuredly true
Only one destroys fatal womb as good
Making us, unworthy, eternally bloom

Years gone, The Heavens dropped manna
John The Baptist, baptised with water
No one, Heavenly, expected to do similar
For, world, then, expected Elijah
JESUS alerted he'd been and gone asunder
Doomed, expecting descending Heavenly Master
Most, expecting JESUS' return
Showing, needing Heavenly rebirth
Own fingers, likely to burn
Who's expecting descendants from the skies?
Revisit where we heard the lies !!!
For, there would be carcasses for flies
What can one see in the clouds?
I ask the eagerly awaiting crowds
Not the place for Heavenly clout
What does one see in the clouds?
Should be clothed in Heavenly shrouds
With wisdom, on eternal grounds
What does one see in darkened clouds?
Angels ascending, descending on their rounds?
Wished I could feel their lovely gowns
To every cloud, a silver lining
Our Be-attitudes should yield positive findings
But it cannot be, with engrained lying

Heavenly Innovation Call

If 3310 Phone was revolutionarily good
Smart phones, now in use
They too, soon, would be dead news
Oh yes, 3310 was a revelation
But there is better innovation
Should we refrain, face liquidation?
So, it is with Heaven
Should try and with Him, be level
Stepping quickly on accelerating pedal
For, from mother's wombs
We carry "Holy Books"
But, won't taste prophets' foods
From birth unto pathetic deaths
We're "steadfast worshippers"
Where are the awarded fathers?
We're meant to be brothers and sisters
Yet, lip service, we provide, for hatred
Where are The Heavenly innovators?
Required to be brothers and sisters
Displayed, like, when children
We need innocence, as leaders, brethren

We're supposed to be one brother and sister
Yet, Rabbi, Imam, Pastor etc., never nearer
Who then, is this other leader?
When talking of loving one another

Yet, division in behaviour
Who, then, is this other father?
Priding in ceaseless fasting, prayer
Performing angelically to others as redeemer
Who then, the other conductor?
Following spiritual beliefs to the letter
Quoting quotes, as coordinates the teacher
Show, then, the other controller
When JESUS spoke about raising stones
Was referring to all like me, so low
Yet, with emptiness, we boast
World, in massive prison home
Knowing only what it upholds
Hence, good, never whole
We're all fragile, raw egg
And like stone, unaware, needing help
With humility could be of good use instead
What does clay, stone, know, to be of any use?
How good is world, prisoner, headline news?
Let's re-awake, paying Heavenly deuce
Surrendering, not, to killers
Who would remove us from pillars
And throw us to alligators
Let's not be swayed by pranksters
Who promise skyscrapers
But are, indeed, squatters
Be weary of the deceitful
Who appear bountiful
But we are indeed, very pitiful
Refrain from their sweet talks

For they are growing stalk
Part of massive stock
For The Lord is forever King
In Him, everlasting wing
Flies us from wicked one's sting
He is eager for you
To finally say, phew
I belong where I'm due

Who claims to be the best?
Let him fear the worst
For the bubble can only burst
Let the one who acclaims being best
Be weary of ensuing test
He wouldn't want the title, first
To be best, portraying Heaven, with zest
Best, hasn't yet seen a contest
To acknowledge the one who purrs
Who are dancing the floss?
The dance of The Heavenly Boss?
Careful, not to fall on the floors
There is unleavened bread
And a loving dread
Which do we prefer instead?
There is unleavened bread
And a lying joyful stead
Which do we like to spread?
Yes, unleavened bread
A sweet-and-sour tread
Which will be our word?

Worthy unleavened bread
A sweet-and-sour trend
This is our world !!!
Salvation message, not learnt
Accredited, as earned
To whom, diligently, yearned

Exemplifying Almighty's Rejuvenated, Nature
Would be seismic surprise, not winning here
Lying on the bed made by Heavenly nurture
As Heaven, provides, above smidgen of hope
Graciously, we would easily, more than cope
Duly reaping what Heaven has readily sown

The Heavens, all of us, trolls
Founded in enemy lines, we stroll
According to His indelible scrolls
Who says he is rich?
Let him take a pick
He is not worth a wink
What is being earthly rich?
Let him show his mint
He is not worth slightest bit
The Heavens, not for the affluent
No one has money, to influence
We're only a deadly congruence !!!
We who glowed in the streets
Upholding the apostles creed
What has become of our fleet?
Yes, we, who glowed in the streets

No mercy for anyone who pleads
Are we now sadly on our knees?

We, champions on the streets
Going places in stringent beliefs
How come, no longer on our feet?
We swore by everything in the streets
Into highest places, were beamed
How come we seriously seethe?
Yes, we controlled the streets
Quieting everything that humbly bleats
A blind eye to those who badly bleed
Yet, to The Heavens we dutifully feed?
Thought portrayed for all to seed
But, sadly, deny poor, basic needs
The Heavens not for the pompous
Disguised, Heavenly religious
Can only be unidentifiably disastrous
Abstain from the ominous
Who drive others envious
Truly unreasonably callous
With no room for the glamorous
Whose lives, nearing momentous
Now, even more so obvious
Because it is the head of the never serious
Whose blessings are so dangerous
And their prayers, very treacherous
Heaven, definitely, not for the pompous
Living, so precarious
Now, evidently, so traitorous

Heaven, no place for the pretentious
Leading others treasonous
Every word, badly hazardous
Undoubtedly, Heaven displaces the ostentatious
Replica, so duplicitous
Every iota, just perilous
The Heavens, never for the pompous
Who live, sliding, precipitous
Because forever rebellious
Who is free of this, want to know ?
Who is clean, the hands to show ?
All claim Heavenly seeds, yet do not sow !!!
All empty, yet pompous
Sadly, singing same chorus
Making The Heavens, overly, furious

Heaven doesn't favour haughtily conspicuous
Let him prove with his bonus
A double agent with the hideous
Who is not Heavenly, pompous?
When, actively enrolled with the monstrous
Heavenly call would be horrendous !!!
Who has managed from being imperious?
Who is justifiably not heinous?
Disaster would be enormous
What makes us happy?
The money tapped in?
Or the accolades we're adoring?
What do we really enjoy?
Best, in academic job?

Or marriage proposal, managed to pop?
The wife, husband, business, children?
Thinking, all from Heaven?
Showing off, therefore, as blessing?
All world, below par
Not even mediocre
In Him, all, dangerously afar
So, helping as Undercover Boss
Who better than the Overall Lord?
He, is truly Tops
When we're surprised by one
And gives more than what we want
From Him, no better grant
When rewarded by one
With us, to have fun
Yes, us, and entire clan
Who is prepared, let him hear?
Whose life, is certainly dear?
Will serve Almighty all year
The keen to listen, let us hear
Proving that, regarding sin, we're clear
Let him, therefore, declare
Who, not hard at hearing, let him hear
The Heavens, he must fear
For He is carrying a massive tear
Who has an ear, to listen here
We know we all have an ear
Let us not continue, a dead deer
It should not be, vanilla response
Carrying a serious riposte

A life and death issue to retort
We treat The Heavens as an ass
Yes, thinking He is nuts
For, by the devil, we are stung

Who eats from dirty dishes?
No matter the meal and drink fizzes
Wouldn't taste, not what one wishes
Not eating from clean crockeries?
Nothing good it garnishes
Everything in there, it rubbishes !!!
Who brunches from dirty dishes?
With all the best fishes
Illness it accomplishes
We all dine from unworthy ceramics!!!
Would you offer to accomplices?
Imagine what it publishes !!!
We enjoy lunches from dirty dishes
Confirming what the enemy relishes?
What is it, it establishes?
Who munches allergic recipes?
What is it that it relinquishes?
We'll know what it extinguishes!!!
Who eats unhealthy specialities?
Do we know what it distinguishes?
We'll know what it refurbishes !!!
Heaven, a respecter of channels
For He comes down to our levels
Constantly using humans as vessels
The Heavens, respecter of persons

But not, devilish versions
Of supposed Heavenly sessions
When married to The Heavens
Yet married to someone else
What really is the process?
Married to The Heavens
Acquires Heavenly Status, eternal pardons
Privilege, momentous, without burdens
Sadly, all have signed contracts
To heavily remain in contact
With everything world constructs
All have signed contracts
Worldly desires, never to distract
From earthly innovations, never to retract
We have all signed contracts
The worldly link, never to detract
Keenly on informative extracts
Yet, all assume signing contracts
To Heavenly remain intact
Not realizing, being expats!!!!!
Who has guts to resign?
From deadly worldly design?
Telling devil, no longer his pre-sign

Who has zeal to resign?
From being part of evil enzyme
Ready for end time
Who is prepared for Heavenly relay?
To forward baton without delay
Part of a momentous Heavenly display

Who is heeding warnings?
Withdrawing from satanic warmings
Pictured in Heavenly drawings
When people lose lives
Rest get traumatized
But who saves from being dramatized?
When people lose lives
Of real causes, we lose sight
Tracing from source, where it all lies
Psychologists, trying to stop lies
Without knowing root of human lives
Avoiding surface lies, itself, a lie
Cannot solve deep problems
Applying trivial emblems
Bearing no Heavenly semblance
Applying a lie detector
Never like measuring with protractor
A lie has deeper indicator
The use of lie detector
Not like flying helicopter
Not Heavenly projector
What we call truth, lies
Not resolving underlying slides
Never, anyway, been on our side
We need robust underpinning
Leading to Heavenly winning
First steps to eradicating sinning
Never truth, in filthy lives !!!
Truth not acquired on silver-plata
Requires revamping lifestyles

Never truth, in filthy lives !!!
Amassing dirty fortune, dimes
Should be weary of Heavenly dice
Truth does not mix with dirty lives !!!
Like chalk and cheese, will surely dive
Will never join hands to dine!!!
Listening to scholars regarding bible studies
Tells shallow minds, these entities
Trying, interpreting Heavenly activities
Never interpret Heaven with carnal minds!!!
Should dig into Heavenly finds
To know True Christmas pines

Cannot interpret Heaven with carnal minds
Incurs astronomical fines
Making us drank on strong wines
Hence, worldly best only teach
But, good, cannot reach
Requires more than just preach
Always, an honour
To properly seek this splendour
Envisaging True Heavenly odour
Roadmap to real understanding
Who has that Heavenly standing?
To receive, deliver true interpreting
When people cannot ride tricycles
Imagine, attempting riding unicycles
What heavy tumbling dazing cycle !!!
If I cannot ride a tricycle
How can I even think of a unicycle?

How crazy we are, in sad triangles !!!
This is us today, fascinating !!!
Football shot targeting airborne plane, mesmerizing !!!
Fishing by hand at deep-seas, captivating!!!
Our best strategic move to achieve !!!
Sadly, leaders not aware of this mischief !!!
Who has nous, out of this siege?
One chasing plane taxiing on tarmac!!!
Would never be on marks
Best thing world has done!!!
Professionals strict dos and don'ts
Spiritual strategies, not even amateur, tops
Needing better accepted trumps!!!
What Heavenly abolish, we embrace
With deceitful guile to prove case
Not knowing, works, finally, win the race
Billions of congregations, not Heavenly instructed
Featuring two year old riding tricycle, appreciated
Cannot use on motorways, at best, mutilated
Preachers focused preaching, unfruitful
Instead of making Heaven say, "this is beautiful"
Ending with everything deceitful
Preach the word to every corner of the world!!!
Apart from Heavenly, who does well?
Pockets, filled, in name of Heavenly Bells!!!
Rags to riches, looking at the Leader
JESUS says, copy me as I do, My Father
Who leads this way as Heavenly Master?
Most of congregation, have nothing

Leaders, oblivious to how they find something
Let alone, make decent living

The "Holy Books" tell us what everyone did
If cannot do good, He accepts, we are kids
Using Holy Throne to dupe, including His !!!
Hits numerous blows below the belt
Sending shock waves, so badly felt
Should come out of it quickly, with zest !!!
The lack, implies, no remorse
Dealing us badly from evident reports
Who wants out of evil doors?
Yet, we think we work, blessed
Needing rethinking, for being cursed
Our lives, constant pathetic mess !!!
Working for anything required, slavery !!!
Like imprisoned royal at quarry !!!
A king, working, in pantry!!!
The "Bastard", coming a thief !!!
Who really has this true belief?
To receive ultimate relief !!!
The "Bastard" coming in balaclava !!!
Who, the detective, Mr. clever?
To spot confirmed seasoned robber"
"Bastard" coming, a gangster
Who calls himself the bouncer?
He looks nothing, a monster
The Lord, coming, a gangster !!!
Who calls himself, pastor?

Any legs to withstand disaster?
King of Kings, coming, a gangster
Where, do I stand, barrister?
World, nothing, but mere prankster
Which judge fits, onto Him, pass judgment?
What's been decided, oh you government?
Who has clout, declaring commandment !!!
The goal posts, shifted !!!
World, long, been twisted
Heaven, protects His, from tricksters
Congregation, now, one
All knowing what they want
Readied for what is done
We reap what we sow
What future, prepared for souls?
Measure of attitudes, displays so
Majority won't budge
Qualification, displayed with badge
Heavenly trail, not, enjoying chocolate fudge
For, in it, should totally indulge
Active daily, constantly involved
Requirement, definitely not insult

Heard all before
Continue hearing, with all
Aware, what we're doing, we retort !!!
Heard all before
The oblivious, it would befall
We will always stay at the fore
Forget it, heard all before

In life, always, a fall
To ancestors, would call
What we have, our hands gained !!!
Believing ours, God made
Least to max, we'll always claim!!!
Forgetting, we breathe for free
Feeding freely from trees
Abuse, blocking Heavenly dreams
In fact, not every land, habitable!!!
Therefore causing many, uncomfortable
By decisions, to Heaven, unhospitable!!!
Exposure to inexplicable dangers !!!
Sailing to dangerous breakwaters
The moon, mars, now, conceivable targets !!!
What is world all looking for?
What are we running from?
Reaching these, thinking top form?
What is world keenly looking for?
Creator, these, does various forms
Yet, pleading with us, not using force
What are we, eagerly, looking for?
Seeking places to tour?
Or away from here, above the law
What are we surely looking for?
Somewhere clean, sins, to possibly pour?
Or transit, looking for more
What are we truly looking for?
Place, sacred, closer to God?
Or somewhere, with more valuable ore
What are we really looking for?

If we knew we could get there without cost
Better still, create some, to be with love ones, and all
Every good out there, in us!!!
Heavenly Kingdom in us, more than a hut!!!
Should enjoy Him, cleansing heart

Dying World

Rather, stuck on false perceptions
No, to constructive corrections
Wherefore, therefore, required perfection?
Ignorantly stuck on wrong perceptions
Refusing to budge from imperfections
Being confirmed by religious derelictions
Deeply sucked into religious perfections
Hence, facing Heavenly repercussions
Not realizing, they're dire directions
Get out of this fragile world, dying!!!
Dying worldly attitude, inferno, all frying
The worm is turning, all crying
World, soon, full of dying souls
For in transit, others particulars, we stole
From missionaries, all are sold
Losing trendy Heavenly composition
Feeding on worldly revolution
Loving innovative decomposition
World, sadly stuck on dearth of perfection
Owing to religious outmoded interpretations
Finding all, in pathetic insertions
Should empty dead self

For The Heavens, to us anew, serve
Following, Prodigal son's steps
Heavenly methodology, we've all botched !!!
Because, level required, we've not notched
Deliberately refused, being torched !!!
Self-righteousness, into abyss, be tossed
For allowing devil, who us, has bossed
Heavenly goodies, therefore, pathetically lost
We, formed in image of Almighty King
Bossed, to things we were not akin
Reduced to role of evil's mannequin
Formed in image of Almighty King
Now actively servants, we are keen
To serve deceitful one, readily plead
Formed in image of Almighty King
Undoubted heirs, next of kin
On whom Heaven Foundation underpins!!!
Oh yes, created in image of Almighty King
In time, ordained, queen
Paraded around in palanquin
Now, clutching on straws
Excited, going where evil draws
Praying steadfastly, Heaven's attention it draws
In God's image, Heavenly righteousness
Yes, living accordingly, in Heavenly perfectness
Like in Adam, having ultimate blessedness
Yet, fasting, prayers, just don't count !!!
Not even sea-level, does it mount !!!
Nowhere near Heaven, does it sound!!!

Fasting, prayers, all year round
Like listening to wicked one's sounds
So, Heaven, for our hearts, always pounds
In fasting, prayers, have we vowed
Thinking with that, Heaven we bow !!!
Leading deeper into worldly row
In fasting, prayers, thinking we're right
Not conscious we're losing fight
For, road to Heaven, surely is tight !!!
Fasting, prayers, presumed some might
In haughtiness, leading all out of sight
Of The Heavenly sacred, eternal light
Fasting, prayers, we'll always have
Out of our troubles, will never carve
For no good, really, we always starve
Turning to fasting, prayer, meditation
Again, never remuneration !!!
Who orders it as resolution?
These two strategies, always been
Patriarchs, Judges, always seen
Beyond these, brethren, Heaven deems
Because prayer, not, word spoken
Assumed spiritual token
From Heavenly angels, have we stolen !!!
Prayer, everything done, before call
So, Heaven already knows, before talk
Why, we always greatly fall
Should be connected first to Heaven !!!
For deeds, to Him, untaintedly level
Thanking Him, not talking like mad men

Fasting, prayer, meditation
Only Heavenly works with dedication
Directed with angelic inclination
We think we know, because we "worship" !!!
Evidently, something wrong, in courtship
Should manage, full steam ahead, midship !!!
Heaven must be King, in hearts !!!
Must be done, and fast
No other strategies or tact,
Heaven must be King in our hearts !!!
He does not do cold or halves !!!
Having warned, to spit out !!!
Heaven must dwell as King in our hearts !!!
With works showing as fact
No other formula to this pact!!!
He has alerted, Heaven inside us
Should follow His institutional prospectus
To gain The Heavenly expected impetus
The Way to The Heavens, is this
Seeking The Way that is His
Without which, all in deadly ditch
When The Lord finally takes His own
What becomes of the "Too Known?"
Into evil stance, they would have grown

Arise, Deceived Asleep World

Who doesn't know worldly time?
We cannot tell what's in line
Can't even read warning signs

The Creator, way ahead of game
All in a blink, does He tame
With Him, there is no same !!!
We acknowledge by mouth, without practice
Time up, He follows overlooked notice
With Him, there is more than justice
So, arise world, so deceived
For nothing left to be retrieved
When loving ones deceased
Therefore arise, from sleep fading world, arise
To avert Heavenly driers
Bringing food to fruitful carriers
Arise, fading world, arise
To achieve Heavenly heights
Prepared as ordained rights
Arise, eroding world, arise
To save, though it looks tight
For this world's fast losing might
Arise, from deep sleep, arise
We, with the foresight
To receive what, for which, is priced
Arise, creepy world, arise
Avoid foolish pride
To reclaim eternal price
Arise, tumbling world, arise
Mount your Heavenly prize
Which no one, to us, ascribes
Thus, arise, you world, arise
Whatever, whoever we think, on our side
Can only produce a downward cite

Therefore arise, sleepy world, arise
For whatever makes us thrive
Will cause us nothing, but strife

Hence, arise, dying world, arise
To redirect wrongs into rights
That prevail in Heavenly sights
Let's heed advice to arise, world, arise
Awake the fallen giants!!!
Originally of Heavenly tribes
Again, arise, quickly, world, arise
Yes, The Heavenly trail beset with trials
The thought of it, means inevitable triumphs
Nothing to fear, world, so arise
Whatever against us, opposition contrives
To wear back, The Heavenly attires
I summon you to arise, fading world, arise
To The Heavens, in determined strides
To attain the optimal prize

SHOULD EAGERLY GRAB, THIS SACRED PRICE
ARISING HURRIEDLY FROM DECAYING PRIDE
NONE WORTHIER, THAN THIS UNIQUE PRIZE
HEAVEN'S HEIRLOOM, EVENTUALLY SEALED
DISPLAYING, A CHILD'S ATTRIBUTES INDEED
ENSURING, THIS, TO ALL, NOT JUST A DREAM
GLOWING IN QUALITY, ETERNAL, FOUNTAIN
YES, HEAVENLY ACTIONS MAKE US BLOSSOM
JESUS OVERSEEING INEXPLICABLY WINSOME
SO, AWAKE, UP, AWAKE, LET US, ALL, WORLD

CHAPTER SEVEN

Religion What Have You Done?

Rebirth Wish

Wished, I was a child again
To correct mistakes I made
For, I tried all sorts, to no avail
Because, when the wheeler dealer deals
And the dealer seeker wins
What is the value of vanity?
All have a Lord
The one diversely called God
Where, though, is the awe?
As all are born, sinned
At best, pinned deeply into religion
Yet, with deep brotherly inhibitions
With all having ambitions
Portraying best religions
But, so empty in our missions
Preachers preaching teachings
All sorts of important meetings

Yet, ultimately, nothing Heavenly yielding
Wished, I was a child again
For Heavenly birth-right to regain
Everything here, now, staid

Daily, the groans, moans and growls
Rigorously unto Greatest of Thrones
Wherefore, then, are thy gold?
All have burning desire
Proving to have the fire
For what then, do we tire?
All, seeking blessings
Following on what they are pressing
Not knowing who is resourcing
When blessing is having money
Silver and gold, Peter says, not having
Preferring heeding Heavenly call, for pardon
Silver and gold, Peter never had
But, genuinely gave, in whom, he is clad
Heavenly JESUS, making Heaven glad
Silver and gold, Peter, brethren, denounced
For having JESUS, world, de-crowned,
Hypocritical world, then, decried
Silver and gold they did not have, empty
Demonstrating level of integrity
Empty world declares such, pity
Silver and gold, not, they boast
What was ignored, on some coasts
World, from the deep, to our abodes
Silver and gold, no, worthless

Having acquired ever revered, priceless
Let the ignorant deem it timeless
In Heavenly walk, they did not need
For JESUS, to whom, world, now plead
Without whom, would endlessly bleed
Silver and gold they never craved
In JESUS, abundantly in grace
Imposters crave to pathetic graves
Silver and gold, they saw as vanity
Gaining, instead, priceless rarity
Religion cherishes, as prosperity
Silver and gold, world see as property
When freely could have gained novelty
Apostles authentic, sacred originality
JESUS, who also lived, left, with empty
Required to show world, graceful sympathy
Having received from Father, all authority
This silver and gold, source of fatal malaise
Killing all, with batons, in spiritual relays
Wish world would awake, to correct mistakes

Loving silver, gold, kingdoms, marriages, been thrown
Into broken, derelict homes, disowned
"Success", platform for preachers, angelic, revoked
Selling fake word, the genuine gave for free
Wolves dressed in skin of sheep
Oh, how, some, would ceaselessly weep
What therefore is this blessing?
Lack of knowledge, all, perishing
Answer lies in reconnecting Heaven

Worldly seeking, researching, a disguise
Heavenly ones we just despise
In our faces, yet, we couldn't see right
All, idol worshippers before The Lord
Keeping evil inside, never, Heavenly tops
Always worrying, we are our own con
For, day and night, loving to pray
Our own souls our lovely prey
Feeding lavishly on deadly spray
Whispering and yelling into clouds
Thinking Heaven hears all and shouts
Only, truly, going around-and-about
Our mediums, forecasters, astrologers
Foretelling the weather prospects
The Messiah's coming, no one deciphers
Doctors losing patients
Architects losing structures
Who has profound lectures?
Looking up into the sky
Expecting more than birds that fly
Crocodile tears, all the cry
We look up into the sky
Gazing intently like a spy
What really, are we trying to imply?
As we command the sky
Expecting Heaven with a smile?
Nothing but tears we'll only cry
It doesn't help looking up into the skies
Hoping to see JESUS The Christ
Which one then, we say, live in our hearts?

Self-righteousness devouring in droves
Like medication taken overdose
I know-my-right syndrome, all decompose
Forsake not the assembly of the saints
All claiming to have been saved
Yet, live on the way the devil paves
Spirit-filled but not perfect
Missing church, meaning defect
Who knows how to, sins, detect?

We are Spirit-filled, but carnal, human
Deceptive angels capturing minds
Living like Kings on meat and wine
Going to Heaven with bloodied hands
Like deceitful farmer without a land
Not even cutlass in his palm
All yearn for some fame
Playing the same old game
Which to Heaven is very stale
All show off, as able to stand
In respective religious stance
Without a steady rubber-stamp
If there is an evident gloom
Not showing in our mood
Yet, all heading to doom
All the days of our lives
Deeper in sin we duly dive
Not knowing teachings are all lies
But The Lord's, He surely owns
Nothing, no one from Him withholds

A second left, you're on His throne
Daily and yearly, He does, would protect
Like apostles, available, to perfect
He never breaks, right to the end
We do not realize we are blind
Mostly at our deaths do we find
Too late, cannot rewind
Hence, we need that Heavenly rebirth
To safely navigate, eventually, berth
Mothers, mourning catastrophic deaths
All are of same character
Gossipers of equal measure
Where-in the Godliness in each other?
When The Heavens strike
And with Him we are in line
Why the inconsolable fright?
Nothing matters in this world
None of value, safe, His word
To The Heavens, we should wed
The world needs to learn
But the knowledge we must earn
Who has the nerve to make the turn
The world requires a leader
Who bears traits of Heavenly splendour
With the sweet aroma of divine odour

No "Holy Book" Answers

Religious "books" are in parables
Who aligns with these puzzles?

For Heavenly appreciated dazzles?
The world is in a terrible daze
Religions don't live Heavenly phase
Playing catch-up, on previous maze
Who is wise enough to interpret vision?
Without displaying Heavenly mission?
Because sins are not in remission
When Heavenly baking is erased
Because we are unholy crazed
Where, the everlasting Heavenly Grace?
Who knows, value of life?
Who really has that in mind?
While flowing with worldly rhymes
Definitely, more than delight
To be accredited a lifeline
A wonderful chance of a lifetime
Who has the nature of the Lord?
Who wears the crest of God?
Like refined water from humble pot
Where is the brotherly life?
When evil against another, so rife
Sniffing out for right time to strike!!!
Thinking religious routines are right
Yet, daily talking about plights
The slightest wobble, there is fright
Oh, wherefore, the faith?
Nothing but terrible augmented fame
Walking down evil's isle, so frail
When the rich think they're rich
Clueless, that they're be-twitched

In this world, which, is in bits
Some, awakening to the thought
That the sought for, is nought
To be worshipped, indeed, not
Religion, to Heaven, a presumption!!!
Offering not true redemption
But, who gets out of this assumption?
It only pulls the world down
Spiritually, looking like a clown
When alerted, does at least, frown
Walking around thinking, we belong
Not to the Heavens, are we thronged
Even flowers' lives, very long
Who is ready to help?
Who can save himself?
Let alone save someone else

Another questioning place
Who has a point to make?
Let him start from his own pace
Who wants to take the lead?
Let him be the first to plead
To be able to breathe indeed
Belonging to a religion, is okay
So long as you lie in wait
For Heaven's crucial eternal date
Religion, excellent for worldly morals
Following path of accepted, ethical
Cleaning up our streets, which is magical !!!
Talking about The "Holy Bible"

What are the principles?
How good are today's disciples?
In the case of The "Holy Koran"
How close to Heaven could we run?
Who has guts to carry the can?
When it comes to The "Holy Torah"
Evidently, with it can't go far
Who is smart enough to go any farther?
None takes righteous bait
Out of religious leisurely gaits
To the shores of Heavenly gates
Absolutely nothing against religion!!!
All about new beginnings
To land Heavenly evergreens
Religions enlighten about some Almighty
Then, consequences of Heavenly notoriety
To choose between satanic and Heavenly eternity
But, not designed Heavenly tools
For, leaders shoved messengers into tombs
Yet, crying wolf, thinking, they, are rather good
Therefore, we are at our wits end, seeking resolutions
But fed with archaic crumbs of postulation
In pursuit of approved Heavenly indoctrination
Who carries year one books daily into adulthood?
Which doctor has medical books following him too?
Evidently, without content in us, carrying, Holy Books
Who studies curriculum during exams?
Too late, for teacher to have time
Seriously, attending to other pressing tasks
Exam time, not time to discuss curriculum

Would be left behind, with swinging pendulum
Guaranteed, we will never be on the podium
Not time to discuss curriculum
Long ago, had we, this memorandum
Being accustomed to the modus-operandum

Who takes notebooks to exams room?
Expecting Messiah, actions should portray mood
So, needing them means, like the five women, fools
Who takes notes to exam hall?
Should have learnt all before !!!
Wrong time to make this call
Having notebooks in exam room, cheating !!!
When caught, consequence not pleasing
No one to defend, all alone, left weeping
Making this move in exam room, conscious wrong
Will not save, not Heavenly norm
To be withdrawn, won't be allowed to perform
"Holy Books" assumed elevation into The Way of Life
We, living according to Heaven, without lies
But, time immemorial, we use them as bribes
Way of Life, not divided, secular, religious, no
But, in focus with Heaven, direct from Throne
Where we all desire to, finally, make our home
So, knowing who we individually, are
Makes, very promising start
Hopefully, handpicked as one
Understanding who we are in Heavenly responsibility
Undermines our standing in community
Which does not come with pomposity

Acknowledging one another in the community
A true sign of who we really are, with divinity
Which is never chaotic in society
We should individually know who we are first
To appreciate each one's role best
Realizing that the least, rather, The Greatest

Personal Action Required

Oh, what a dawn !!!
Definitely not a yawn !!!
When from the lot, you are drawn !!!
To throw down the gauntlet
On such a thrilling project
With Heaven, who will us, protect
Who is prepared to gain Heavenly respect?
Him, The Heavens would select
To provide the eternal outlet !!!
Who is ready to throw down the gauntlet
The Heavens would never reject
Seeking who, from the devil, are ready to defect
Again, who relinquishes evil, fully prepared
The evil forceful activities, finally, neglect
And, to eternity, duly connect?
Who stands up, throwing down the gauntlet
And into the abyss all sins downed, reflect
Forever, from the enemy, eject
Who dares to woeful anomalies, redress?
Him, shall He, from the masses, detect
To dodge the imminent Heavenly bullets

Who stands out throwing down the gauntlet?
When nothing good, activities, yielded
And, of evil's endeavours, not circumspect

Heaven wants to know who can climb
When onto roads end, clamped
Accepting, truthfully, Heaven does not carp
Who wants to throw down the gauntlet?
And in The Heavenly eyes, appeal as perfect
Operating as a Heavenly approved hornet
World under siege, who stands out?
With swashbuckling desire, making oneself proud
Onto everything Heavenly, pounce
This, best chance of a lifetime!!!
Who, really, has a dime?
To miss out, out of sight
Yes, a chance of a lifetime !!!
To play the incredible chime
With the angelic brethren, humbly rhyme
Please, seize this chance of a lifetime
This, indeed, is your prime
Enjoying dialogues with Heaven, not a mime !!!
Who wants to miss this chance of a lifetime?
When even diamond we cannot mine
To have eternity, to call, all mine
Not just a holiday sign
But, to be better than our evergreen pine
As, planted by the River Tyne
To whom do we pay homage?
What is our heritage?

Is it the renowned Heavenly stage?
We need sacrificial tinge to wake-up
Yes, with the Heavens, hurriedly make-up
Needing a revolutionary shake-up
Why is there so much sleep?
Drugged into a steep
Deeper than the ocean deep
Where are all the leaders?
Not to mention the preachers
Supposed national fatherly kingmakers
From birth to death
We've been a threat
To our very own selves

Carrying on from birth
All the filthy dirt
With which we have zealously berthed
Where are the leaders?
The committed able runners
Not even fit to be pacesetters
Who is the athlete?
Who, at the gun won't compete?
If competing, in direction completely opposite
Where is the one ?
Who knows how to run?
But does not know a race track
Where is the runner?
Who knows not a starter
To be a possible winner?
I want to know the runner

Who claims to be better
No doubt, Heavenly prophets, faster
They are our brothers and sisters
Yearning to see us, winners
From renowned global schemers
Who is the one person?
With the true version?
Carrying on saintly sessions?
One, the world has rejected
Therefore, apparently, so dejected
Because all have sinfully, averted
Who carries mantle of justice?
Forget national statistics
Heaven recognises no worldly academics
Who makes Heaven excited with a masterpiece?
Can only be done in Heavenly peace
Not acquired from worldly rice and peas
All are tricksters
Very astounding fraudsters
Leading all to being deserters
Emptying pockets of the needy
Making their minds so weedy
With lying scythe, they become history
Their tongues, unpardonably, deceived
Obliged, therefore, received
This is brilliant, they have believed
For the devil takes the hindmost
This is what religion posts
Emptying all, physically, spiritually, they boast

No one is perfect !!!
Emphasising, without the milk of human kindness
Oh, if I had my druthers…
But, we all need to work hard together
Looking after one another as the keeper
For starters, on a wing and a prayer
For, the world knows what to do with you
Wishing, could tie you under water, in a canoe
And paddle you far out of human view
Where there would be no chance of a rescue
Both on land and at sea in truth
And no matter the length, depth, search, renewed
Empty like an arid desert
Because the truth, we all desert
The devil uses us for meals and desert

Deceived Shells

Because of our foundation!!!
Founding fathers of nations
Upon what is our reputation?
We've become empty shells
Upon all the renowned research
Nowhere fit for Heavenly shelves
Yes, deceived, very broken shells
Without a value for one to sell
Left to rot like smelly eggshells
Yes, we are broken shells
The meat of value, locked up in cells
Where are the brains to think of ourselves?

Oh, we wasted broken shells
Do we not realize we're under evil spell?
To come out, gladly, eternally, excel?
We need to fight back, broken shells
All flesh, wicked ways, expel
Dealing in Heavenly business shares!!!
Till when, to be of any use, broken shells?
Having filled bellies with strong wine in bushels
Watering mouths, staggering, badly, empty vessels!!!
Can still make it, trampled on, shells
Creating fantastic headlines, bombshell !!!
Unfancied, has gained tops, in a nutshell
If we could have a reflection
Of our state, now, in desertion
Cast away into lengthy detention
World, always pins another with offence !!!
Never managing Heavenly shortfalls, for defence
No use either, staying on the fence
World, cease blaming another with offence
Rather, grab summer holiday travel offers

To have something lined up, in coffers
Let no one decorate another with offence
For this is about global conference
Each, acquiring best Heavenly reference
Cease being embroiled in devoid of offence
For, each, The Heavenly, offends
Hence, requiring Heavenly accorded cadence
We have all been deceived
Into thinking we have truly received

What Heaven requires us to achieve
We have all been deceived
Into believing The Holy Spirit is retrieved
Like a child with Christmas gifts indeed
We've all been seduced
Into inherent traps, confused
Hence, disentangling, not enthused
Do not be concerned about what you're to lose
Focus, rather on being kept in Heavenly loop
After having cut yourself, from evil, loose
One comes back to life under intensive care
Jubilation from well-wishers there !!!
Job, then, begins, for his welfare
One re-awakes in intensive care unit
Doctor, nurse, perform duty
To the joy of adoring entity
Whatever religion, never the matter
All joy, about awoken brother and sister
Now strong enough, causing disaster?
This is who we are !!!
Thinking we're big, but frail, in a corner
Who has any strength, be, deliverer
Heaven, remains The Only Doctor
Nursing, as sole provider
Cleansing us, The Only Protector
Intensive care patient, does not care who gives treatment !!!
So long as the person receives improvement
Allah, God, Fetish,… not issue, but acquiring eternal enrolment
Intensive care patient, I'm not bothered about the doctor
Or the nurse being my carer

Do I even know the domestic worker?
We worry about too many unnecessary things !!!
Instead of seeking concrete Heavenly beginnings
To receive Heavenly accepted finishing
We waste too much energies on useless things !!!
From our homes, to sky-high thinking !!!
Channel them into Heavenly loving awakenings !!!
We are ALL intensive care unit patients !!!
Who require, among others, Heavenly patience !!!
To correlate in The Heavenly ordained patents!!!

Water is good for the body
But, not just pouring it on us, in clothing
Should rather, be drinking it!!!
Water is good for the body
So, throwing it away, thirsty, is shoddy
Showing, we are all brain-foggy !!!
Where are the publications?
What is the value of the dissertations?
The result of our argumentations
The prophets never had these
They maintained Heavenly acclaimed themes
As part of the devoted Heavenly team
To what then is one devout?
A never descending cloud?
Or a custom-made empty shroud?
So, to what then is one devout?
Shouting to The Heavens aloud?
Or pulling all the crowds?
I want to know what we call devout !!!

The sermons on pulpit we mount?
Or what we think makes us proud?
We need to demonstrate, being devout !!!
Is it the monies we manage to stuff out?
Or our wickedness sucked through the spout?
What do we call devout?
Opposing spirituals arguing, what about?
Without living ONENESS, for voluntary turnaround
Devout, starts from who I am, Heavenly
Treated, accordingly, as with hyssop for purity
To gain Heavenly humility
Where everyone is, brother, sister indeed
Demonstrating oneness beyond belief
Example, for others to enjoy fruit of seed
Only Heaven, then, accredits anyone, devout
No Heavenly walker thinks, bets on any count
Very busy, not knowing if he has a couch
To be devout, an honour from above
When a Heavenly angel practices Heavenly love
Sometimes, we find, extremely tough
It is a humbling feeling to be called devout
The apostles, of it, really renowned
We should emulate, being Heavenly loud
World, not required, to verbally expound
But, living, proof, what Heaven propounds
To whoever needs breaking down, compound

RELIGION, HAS TRIED THIS REBIRTH, DREAM, REAL
"HOLY BOOK" ANSWERS NOT EXISTENT, THIS DEAL
FOR, EVERYONE HAS BECOME FOREVER DECEIVED

TO BECOME AS GOOD A WHOLESOME SHELL AGAIN
CORRECTING ERRORS, I, HAVE KNOWINGLY, MADE
ENSURING, BEING HEAVENLY DEVOUT EVERY DAY
UPGRADING, STANCE FOR THE ONE TRUE RELIGION
ACQUIRING, HEAVENLY MATURITY, AND BLOSSOM
IN HIM, BECOMING ASSUREDLY, REALLY WINSOME
HENCE, WAKE UP, WAKE UP, OH COMPLETE WORLD

To what then, is one's hope?
Moses has been accredited his home
Up to each, to be bespoke!!!
To what then is one's hope?
Matthew too, has his home
Up to us, to be hone
What then, is one's hope?
That Heaven descends in a cloak
Sucking all into machines to cope?
Adam, did not know this initially, hope
Because he had all, nothing to decode
We hope, today, being sinfully doped
What is the hope, in hope?
No one to Heaven, operates as a mole!!!
When sins, washed with ever-cleansing soap?
What is our hope ?
For The Heavens, not to call us foes?
Then, should cut off fatal jokes
What do we call hope?
To see The Heavens in our homes
Pleading we return to evil, that's what we hold?

What do we all expect in hope?
To be Heavenly souls?
With achieved objectives and goals?
In heads, JESUS died for our sins !!!
Yet, selfishness cans us into more than tins !!!
Wickedness, envy, hatred, greed, lunge into deeper bins
We've all become vile
Wickedness in us, rife
Anger as bad as bitter bile
So-called religious, don't send right vibes
Deeds, so, pathetically rile
Without possessing, showing, Heavenly lire
If JESUS died for sins, why, crying onto pastors?
Why seeking church answers?
Pastors seek greener pastures !!!
If JESUS died for sins, why, still sinners?
Why, spiritual, emotional, mental stress?
Why, always depressed?

If JESUS died for sins, why needing places of worship?
Easily eaten by evil as turnip
Hence, not showing Heavenly quality tulips
The apostles demonstrated sinless state
In no church did they engage
When they did, they controlled the stage
No one else, again, ever taught them
They, rather, everyone else, taught, thence
For, in them, there was no pretence
Being, the stand-out, real deal
From The Master, they provided Heavenly feel

What they said, did, final and Heavenly real
Target for us, the rest!!!
Some not trying, others doing their best
What comes out of worldly best, least said
This is how, all, expected to live
Heaven, we should, in and out breathe
Under auspices of Heavenly briefs
Yes, needing continuity from there
Comparing apostles, today's, take us nowhere
Nowhere, meaningful, much as we dare
So, who wants to cover himself in glory?
Considering labour is plenty, yet always snoring
To experience encouraged Heavenly roaring
Spirituals, leaders know, they're not solution
Because all they give, pollution
Oh, yes, compounding confusion !!!
Knowing, without eternal answers
For money, they entertain us !!!
Get out, world, of destroyed bunkers !!!
Any failing business, changes tactics
If strategies still not yielding
They completely call it quits
Staying on, means, everything working
According to objective planning
Enjoying luxury, attention, results damning
Anti, the JESUS principles, they daily blurt
With pathetic, shameful flirts
Making deceived, believe they're blessed
Spirituals aware, we're stuck, nowhere to go
So, any interpretation in God's name, goes

Dragging all into massive holes
They are not coached from Heaven's source
With humility, integrity, of apostolic ores
So, when, how will they outsource Overall Boss?
They haven't even considered that stance
Their only target, display financial grandstand
Ignorant to believe, in Lord's blessing, they stand

Truly, Heaven finds us hard to watch
Top to bottom, all downright spoilt
None halting or rotten evil, dodge
All need to rise up to reality !!!
Clean Heaven, demands purity
Arise, world, from burdened iniquity
For He is arisen
Having faced underserved treason
For tangible reasons!!!
He makes entering Heaven, a doddle
Compared with these pathetic wobbles
Who, for Heaven sake, don't have the bottle !!!
JESUS makes entering Heaven a doddle
For sacrificing on the double
Unlike deceitful, leaving us with trouble
Yes, He makes entering Heaven a doddle
Always entering our rubble
So, into Heaven, easily paddle
JESUS makes entering Heaven, a doddle
For being Heavenly supple
Making all, eternally, bubble
Innocent, have lost families, monies, lives…

Even, still, telling deliberate lies
Without remorse, even, looking in the skies
WUOW instead of world, gather what is left
Run, at full pelt
Into opened arms of one who helps !!!
World, portray Heavenly repertoire!!!
That fulfils Heavenly stockpiles
JESUS' acceptable repertory
We need to portray the desired repertoire
That has Heavenly memoires
Looking back on, with fond remembrance
Dreading disasters, fear Heavenly typhoon
Who stops it, won't be a tycoon
Above paper money, stopping Heavenly monsoon
We need favourable swing, with good momentum
Nothing to do with worthless argentum
Quickly, for there is no change in ultimatum!!!

Who is Ready for Change?

Who wants to play a part?
Committing to Heavenly pact
Not about some fun in the park
Who wants to set ball rolling?
For Heaven's encouragement, keep going
For, world is not slowing
Who wants to initiate, reform!!!
For Heaven to help perform
Out of this deadly uniform
Who wants to join, reform?

Out of this dangerous platform
Let him fill The Heavenly forms
Who wants to set the tone?
Heaven ready to strengthen bone
Never to be cold and lone
Who truly has the power?
To withstand the Heavenly mire
Normally undoubtedly dire
To Heaven, who wants to be a friend?
The world cannot be a wrench
World should change dire trend
Who wants to be Heaven's friend?
Should have befriending, open heart, to the end
Enticing all to admit, can't comprehend!!!
Roar of destruction will cause violent violence
More devastating than worldwide Ebola virus
Who isn't prepared to be a variance?
Targeting not group, but whole bundle
Who is lighting required candle?
No hiding in any valley, cave or jungle!!!
Who desires joining Heavenly seeking bundle?
No time to, in this world, dangle
Should all mount humble saddle
What, then, is our sacrifice?
Before the Lord, for it to suffice?
For our hearts are full of distasteful spite
Where is the sacrificial lamb?
Who is prepared to be dumb?
All we have, presented to us, is sham
What happened with Cain and Abel?

When the cane strikes, who is able?
Definitely not fabricated fable
Sacrifices, activities, best efforts, like Cain
Better, hearing, now, alert, taking pain
Before bodies, sadly wane
Heaven does not just desire sacrifice
Not something, world, to improvise
Nor can it be deceitfully compromised
Heaven does not accept every sacrifice
It can't be a camouflage
Should come with Heavenly energise
So, let's not rely on unwanted sacrifice
Which does not Heavenly emphasise
But one, our Heavenly stance fortifies

World, be weary of Cain-like sacrifice
Portraying distinct minimise
But, to Heaven, ably, maximise
Sacrifice, not just, physical present
Deceived into, world, as decent
But which Heaven, undeniably resents
What do we really have to sacrifice?
Apart from getting rid of evil to Heaven suffice
The sacrifice that the humble status satisfies
Should all learn from Cain and Abel
Heaven has no sacrifice requirement tabled
Apart from the open heart, with Heaven, stable
Where are the Heavenly truths?
When we think we are true
Only to gather confused troops

Who on earth knows The Way?
To the Heavenly tray?
Famished for years, without a ray
Who knows the way to The Heavenly Kingdom?
Who even understands Heaven's Dominion?
Not the same passed-on, guess work, opinion?
Who has been told of The Heavenly Kingdom?
Who has the faintest clue of this freedom?
Are we not tired, being Heavenly fandom?
Yes, The Heavenly journey a trail
One way ticket, specific train
Who is ready for the rails?
Yes, The Heavenly journey, a trail !!!
But who wants to be the enemy's prey?
Time to bolt, not to stay and pray!!!
Who wants to join The Heavenly trail?
When all prefer the head, not the tail
But blighted by attitudes, spiritually, pale !!!
Who joins The Heavenly ideal trail?
Cannot stay and become stale
Should try to enjoy The Heavenly steak
For no one, He comes to wait !!!
Ready and steady in the armoury gait
Coded, loaded for the Heavenly gate
Regarding Heaven, forget religions, prisons!!!
Holding captive for one reason
Keeping all, in deadly dungeons
Who is, thinker, outside, box?
When all are sadly, greatly out-foxed
Their lying tongues, stronger than ox

Who has some wisdom outside the box?
Displayed as the Heavenly clean boss
Ensuring, daily, he will, evil, toss
Who can stand up before The Lord?
For Him to say, yes, in you, I'm awed
When to death, we've all been lured
Who is clean before The Lord?
Knowing we're filled with error
With legs before death door

Furnished Followers

Everyone claims worshipping God
Even atheist unknowingly worship the lord
Yet, who, then, communes from His Holy Gourd?
Who will gladly get the nod?
When the Lord makes the call
Knowing very well, we're all wrong
Who will duly get the nod?
When The Heavens cracks the pod
To find out what it has got
Who will surely get the nod?
Ahead of the presumed lot
Lot will rejoice with twin tot
Heaven, looking for one with the nod
Who, surely, is without a dot?
All, swimming in worldly tots
Who are furnished followers?
Apostles proved accredited owners
The Heavenly package, they eventually loaded

Where are furnished followers?
Before our eyes to be shunned as the lowest
For they only encouraged loathers
All are deceptive
Capturing all captive
To sin, we've become receptive
Altering The Heavenly objective
Into everything deadly, sadly, conducive
To evil, very easily submissive
We, and all coordinators
Subdued Truth, into remote back burners
Uplifting those who are Heavenly haters
For they, evidently, rule the roost
Ensuring, all succumb to them, calling the tune
Either that, or all rights pathetically refused
For, no one, duly, acknowledges Heaven
From the least to the superintendent
The astute, all Heavenly, downtrodden
Why should it be like this, why, world?
When there is so much, for you, prepared
Which makes the evil one so much scared
Yes, scared that you are a Heavenly Prince
Knowing, you'll no longer admire his prints
And to your rightful place, back there in a sprint
Turn around to your rightful place
The Heavens is calling for a frantic pate
To let go courageously, the devil, to face

Seek ye therefore, first
The Heavenly Kingdom burst

To pass the eternal test
Yes, seeking therefore, first
The Almighty's humility best
And we are sure to never thirst
With Him first, we are leaders
Dictating the pace as mentors
No one overtaking us, runners
All going at each one's pace
Not at the pace of the other's rate
Properly, in unison, co-ordinated race
We note that, it is written, ye
Meaning, individually, we should be
From each of one's deeds
Strategy that ensures, Heaven has arrived
For everyone, of sin, to be deprived
Works indicating, accredited, as complied
Solely, accountability of each
Nothing to do with another's breach
So, even if together, each, impeached
What each needs, for each only
Even if, together in a group, wholly
Everyone, dealt with, SOLELY !!!
What someone does, different from mine
But Heaven, none undermines
Yet, together, focus on individual congruent minds
So, whatever situation or religion,
Operations, under Heavenly conviction
Because of eternal understanding or intuition
Whichever religion, should portray Heavenly innovation
The kind, world seeks, for inspiration

Expressing ultimate reconciliation
Then, world in selfishness, to dial, togetherness
Instead of wickedness, to go, loveliness
Carelessness innovating, in loving, orderliness
Awake, world, wake up to Heavenly peace
Passing all understanding with deeds
The type, Heaven loves, to see, breed
With deeds saying, religion, where is your pride?
Supposed to abolish the divide
Making all, Heavenly unite
Religion, where is your pride?
Having devised own pranks
Appearing as Heavenly strides
Religion before The Lord has no stand
After manoeuvring all into shanks
Judiciously knocking heads into empty tanks
Religion, religion, religion !!!
Supposed guide from originator's institution
Leading into eternal vision
What now, your journey planner?
Supposedly, putting heads together
With viable, case for Heaven to admire

Clueless Religious Leaders

Poor you, supposed government advising teachers
Where are, sacred executive leaders?
Receiving Heavenly guidance, to ministers
Religion, religion, religion, you and ministers

Should admittedly confess
Laid foundation, for worldly mess
Vacating, required post, being quack
Talking and dealing in pathetic stuff
Heaven declares, you're badly stuck
David, Samuel, Jacob and others, shocked
Solomon, making wisdom mistakes, father of wisdom
We have allowed ourselves to be mocked
World relied on you, for protection
Status, driving us into rightful resolutions
Sorting out, every confusion
Supposed to be our sleuth
The ones we approached for truth
Even to alert us of plans of evil troops
Rather you've sadly segregated
Masterfully, relentlessly, scattered
Seeds of death, have you watered
Who, then, is dedicated?
Enough to be vindicated?
To prove he is devoted?
Who has, Heavenly belief?
Proving, ahead is relief
For, long awaited reprieve
Heaven is calling
Hoping, hopefully, He keeps stalling
From disaster, which, would be befalling

Is there one with character?
Slightly resembling Heavenly indenture?
Then, He will not call on, disaster

Years on end, has He waited
At city gates, He has been unabated
Rural folks, accept, being annihilated
Our love for True One, abated
If, at all, ever existed
Who doesn't deserve being decapitated?
Lost sheep of Israel, dissipated
Handywork of religious rangers
Rigorously pursuing them, masqueraders
World, all are vampires !!!
With burning desires
Destroying own Heavenly empires
We are all living vampires
Sucking the weak, we vandals
Rolling all onto belts as vipers
Getting everyone flustered
Lining all up, punctured
Shoving into spinning machines, deflated
Accepted, the truth hurts
In fact, sin, it actually burns
How many desire this lasting turn?
Should ensure, no stone unturned
Yet, none desire facing surgeon
To undergo unwanted churn
None want to face ultimate surgeon
Saving us feeding as reckless pigeons
Eventually thrown into deepest dungeons
The Heavens provide abundant fish
Yet, we daily portray being selfish
Yes, greed, we accomplish

Who has the courage?
Here, my sins Lord, in this carriage
Tired, of this baggage
This is the best of religion !!!!
Beginner, learner, in mono cycling
How good, his balancing?
Can never avoid fateful consequence
Thus, should deeply search, not a glance
Rampage, arriving in an instance
People sleeping in our streets
We do foreign charities
Oh, we hypocrites!!!!
How can we leave homes dirty
When cleaning someone else's daily
We, full of hypocrisy!!!

Preachers preaching for world to repent
Yet, resourced daily from evil's den
Thus, hypocrites, carrying, bigger dents
The world is listing !!!
Very quickly drifting
So badly sinking
Who is the captain?
Stopping boat from capsizing?
Saving people from drowning?
Who is the Heavenly dealer?
Who is that leader?
Who operates as the Pillar?
The world is twisting !!!
Indeed, violently spinning !!!

Fast, going missing !!!
Who is the rock?
Ready to save the lot
From inevitable rot?
Humpty dumpty, is the stage
Yes, its new image
Falling to the grave
Who has the prowess?
To withstand all encounters?
We need The Holy powers
We are all fumbling
Our memoires tumbling
From failed gambling
Who can hear the cry?
The cry of the fly
As hard as we try
We are nothing but poison
Carried in our bosoms
Overtaken our whole persons
The Heavens has picked up the bow
All wired up on death row
Awaiting flight of the arrow
All are of doubt
In a never-ending bout
Without a referee to do the count
Should avoid what is foul
Stopping, engaging in useless row
Never considered Heavenly bow
All, in a mix
Needing the Heavenly fix

From this undulating devouring jinx
Who has the mantle?
To light the candle
To lead out of this jungle?

North, South, East, West
No one wears, Heavenly crest
Claiming, yes, I'm the best!!!
North, South, East, West
No one claims the first
To galvanize the rest
North, South, East, West
Who is pleading as the worst
To wear The Heavenly vest
Who from North, South, East, West?
Who admits, being a pest
Requiring, Heavenly humble nest
Again, North, South, East, West
I want to see the one with Heavenly zest
Achieving the united quest
Yeah, all over the world
Who is clean enough, saying, yes
"Father speak thy servant heareth !!!"
Being last, for us, the best result
For most are outside Heavenly resorts
According, truly, to all reports
Our sins, so deeply rooted !!!
Before the cry, not even mooted
Far into the ocean deepest, we're routed

Sins are so deeply rooted
Requires lots to be uprooted
Almighty, alone, a twinkle, gets them booted
For, when man tells you kiss the bride
If truly we kept our dignified pride
Equally part of the executioner's ride
So, what is marriage?
A chewing gum, which eventually fades
So mouth requires another sweet taste?
What, then, is marriage?
Meeting ones, from whom to suck advantage?
Or the mix, not Heavenly founded, ending in carnage
I mean, what is marriage?
What sexual drives dictate?
Or legality in which we engage?
Why, then, pandemonium in marriages?
From slums to cottages
Yes, from caves to palaces
If this marriage, Heavenly ordained?
Why do we see so much pain?
One chosen, the other maimed?
Worldly marriages have their merits
Nothing to do with Heavenly nuances
Giving some pluses at certain perils

So, again, what is marriage?
An understanding between two people
As long as they are a couple?
Who calls himself single?
Many claim they are

Without knowing they aren't
Who says he is lone?
No one is really alone
Being connected to the soul
Who claims being single?
We are all controlled by an inkling
Which is very powerful to resist
Marriage isn't what we think
Two people raising kids
Hoping they become queens and kings?
It isn't the "till death do us part"
Requiring us to be rather smart
But providing a longer lasting spark
Ultímate marriage, The Heavens orchestrates
Dos, don'ts, wants, needs, He dictates
Ensuring daily, we have what it takes
Yet, what God puts together
No one puts asunder
What then, is He a liar?
Divorces like changing running stomach nappies
Love bites like deadly rabbies
From generation on end, affecting babies
Our appetite despise Heavenly cookies
Taking our chances with the bookies
Not knowing we're not even rookies
We've torn out the real cook book
Disliking the aroma and its look
Displaying fasting, to Heavenly food !!!
No, it isn't funny !!!
The day isn't sunny !!!

It doesn't augur well for mummy
No, it is not at all funny
Not, good news for daddy
Nothing to be left for shrinking tummy
Even, now, so late in the day
Time yet, to stake a claim
Who is ready to make a name?
Who reads without alphabets !!!
A mandatory step-by-step
Without which we can't progress!!!
Is there anyone beyond reproach?
One connected to The Heavenly Remote
And with a click, then, on the road?

Who is beyond reproach?
One connected to The Heavenly phone?
And activates accordingly like drones
When there is an action
Countered by a reaction
Who renders the right interaction?
Who is beyond reproach?
One who upholds JESUS approach
Receiving groom's applause, a Heavenly brioche
If one is beyond reproach
Should be one who JESUS downloads
Displaying qualities Heaven beholds
So we don't walk about needy
We do not even know how we became sleepy
Even when, how, to awake, to become weepy
Awake, what do we see?

A world tumbling into the sea
Or one far away, from the ocean-deep?
When ready for work, what do we feel?
A fun day in the fields
Or a planned one for us to steal?
What is the plan for the future?
A children to nurture
To be even more prominent in stature
How serious are we about life?
Building castles for us and the wife?
Or everything at our disposal, live
The thoughts on our mind
A prayer to an unknown God to recite?
Or a plan to execute by the lord of our kind?

SEEK YE FIRST,WORLD, THIS DREAM TO BE REAL
FAR, FROM CLUELESS RELIGIOUS LEADERS' DEAL
FURNISHED FOLLOWERS RUN AND HEAVEN SEAL
READY, THEN, COMPLETE HEAVENLY, ESCAPADE
TO CORRECT GRIEVIOUS MISTAKES I HAVE MADE
ENSURING FINALLY, THERE IS NO VOID IN PLACE
WHICH RELIGIOUS ONE DOES PROVE FAULTLESS?
DAVID ENSURED HEAVENLY, WASNOT CLUELESS
JOSEPH'S PREDICTION HELPED EGYPT, FLAWLESS
HENCE, WAKE UP, WAKE UP, PENNILESS WORLD!!!

For, times have changed !!!
The Commander-In-Chief is enraged
To save, put others in chains
When one, presumably, with wealth

Possibly living, better health
Can they avoid, inevitable death?
Talk of mental health !!!
Imagine then, what comes out as breath !!!
All dressed up, but shambolic spiritual wrecks
As fish out of water
Can only, a short while, flatter !!!
And that is a serious matter !!!
Imagine, fish out of water
Only so much, can we muster
At the mercy of The Ultimate Master
As fish out of water
In the hands of the destroyer
To be cooked by someone's fire !!!
Yes, as fish out of water
Our lives appear almost over
On the last breath, to hold further?
Hm, as fish out of water
That is how vulnerable we are
Until somehow back, deep in the oceans farther
This is our current state
For this joy will not forever give good taste
Overdue time we run to The Heavens in haste
This is our present predicament
No solution, not even from the government
Nothing, no one, apart from Heavenly Parliament
We are all like mouldy blue berries
Meant to be good but no longer healthy
Therefore, no longer fit for bellies
Who are we readying for hosting?

The folks facing dethroning
Or the Heavenly angelic ghosts?
Who do we want to host?
Is it the decaying earthly post?
Or the life and land as the gold coast?
Oh, that we may be part of Him, out of this noose
To call our own, not to lose
The Heavenly path, to find the goose
We hope the goose is beating its wings !!!
To acquire what the world seeks to link
To be acknowledged with Him as Kings
So, to whom do we owe our heritage?
Is it the place of earthly historical date?
Or the eventual spiritual return age?
To whom do we owe our heritage?
Is it the same deadly worldly birth place?
Or the original Heavenly eternal adage?

To whom do we really owe our eternal heritage?
Is it the one who our sins can manage?
Where to add on already burdened tonnage?
With the evil one, continually taunting
Living life, still haunting
Oh, such a state extremely daunting
Making our lives, a fiction
Being in line with the evil vision
Who curtails what we're fishing?
All seem to think we know
Where we intend to go
But will there be for us a home?

This, a Heavenly corruption !!!
So much sin, untold pollution
All facing damning damnation
We should remember to use our heads
To stand us in good stead
Wherever we step
Time to let go of emotions
They are not the final motions
They are, but, temporary erosions
For no one speaks the truth !!!
We do not live by the root
Building our houses from the roof !!!
Yet, who knows this?
That we live in total eclipse
Reading from these Heavenly glimpses
The world has been invaded
The tenancy raided
By unsuspecting invaders
Overtaken by a giant storm !!!
This is beyond the norm
How can we rightfully perform
Who is homeless?
Not the one by the street side penniless
Or loitering because he is worthless
Who, then, is homeless?
Not one seen as drunken hopeless
Or one, unclean, smelling of rottenness
Who really then is homeless?
Not one who is roofless
But one without JESUS

No one, including me, has JESUS' impetus
Hence, looking for place to lay head
Such, is truly, Heavenly blessed
Religion thinks it is complete
Heavenly Kingdom, received
Yet, enjoy only worldly drumbeat

All religion think it is fulfilled
Relating to how it portrays belief
Yet, people don't get reprieves
Making, world believe, it is complete
Nothing before, below or underneath
Exactly what we all need
But no, sadly, leading many dangerous
In mind-set, very autonomous
Truthfully, not agile, predictably monotonous
Holding world in captivity
Marginalised Heavenly inactivity
Yet, thinking, has Heavenly audacity
Sad, so many wanting
Numerous hearts desperately panting
Wasting from ignorant munching
Considering themselves "top dogs"
They eat any hot dog as God
Thinking, worked, socks off
All want this, without Heavenly qualification
Apart from worldly routines and adjudications
No, no songs, verbal upliftment, daily devotions
Remember Samuel and Eli

Prophet Eli, ignored, for Hophni and Phinehas
We sin, pray, thinking He has forgiven us
Christian biggies have no clue about Trinity!!!
Muslims divided in their activity
Judaism, nought, on JESUS' deity
If one was pure before The Almighty
Thus, excluded from vanity
"Holy Books" applauding, worthy of eternity
Nicodemus', example, typical of the reason why
None receive sacred messages, rather, lies
If there was one on whom to rely
Ignorant about being born again
A whole JESUS lecture to regain !!!
Playing catch-up, baseless claim!!!

Who Is the Witness?

Who is the witness?
One in position of weakness?
Or one with first-hand account in joyousness?
I am not a hindrance
No, nor a nuisance
All for Heavenly deliverance
So, who boldly stands out as witness?
One giving accurate information with calmness?
Or one believing, has received forgiveness
Heaven desires to know the witness
One living in fulfilled fearlessness?
Or thinking of worldly fullness?
Wish to know, who calls himself, witness?

Those who tread in pairs?
Or those receiving Heavenly stirs
Let's remove waxes from ear-drums !!!
To hear the beat of The Heavenly drums
Without this, the message, always a conundrum !!!
Quickly, dispose of waxes from ear drums
Appearing like, plenty liquor, you've downed
Hearken, world, before you are drowned
Heavenly worship, not learnt
All have therefore, massive dent
We have to be God-sent !!!
JESUS oozed Godly scent !!!
Despite thinking, he was, foul scent
Delivering what Heaven meant !!!
Apostles demonstrated, required basics
Heaven choose each for specific cases
None, learnt the messages
A witness, one who endures an encounter
Humbly, absorbs subject matter
With allotted time, goes to deliver
Direct communication with The Heavens
Knowing exactly what to do, where stepping
Correctly worships, even if deafening
Walking, aligned with, and within The Lord
Relaying instructions, with deeds as borne
Stepping in footsteps of The Living God
Yes, the witness, even in this worldly law
Must be sure to tell what he saw
Not hearsay, secondary source
First- hand account, originally direct

With secondary, backing-up, as dissert
And Heavenly Seal of Approval, as perfect
A unique individual leading Heavenly lines
Different from protracted deadly lies
Delivering Heavens intentions as timed
Walking **I**n **T**ruth, **N**aturally **E**xpresses **S**aviour's **S**alvation
Who bears credentials of sanctification?
Displaying Heavenly wilderness edification
A witness, not by mouth, but like apostles
Daily walking the talk that resembles
JESUS', with Heaven's confirmed, approval
Called Christians, they never accepted
Happy, being, The Lord's anointed
Accepting, same, would want them rejected

For, with JESUS, they were not equal
And, same mouth, would seek, to them, devour
So, in humility, their cases, rightly resolved
Carrying other peoples' quotes a sad joke
If they wouldn't in worldly courts, hold?
How, before The Heavenly Throne, cope?
No one, protected, by religious group
All walking on same deadly route
Planted deeply in same roots !!!
The apostles brought it to light!!!
Peter completely denying The Christ
Philip asking questions about their lives
JESUS apostles were equally rubbish
They would have been punished

Alongside all, to be completely banished
Again, Saul, Paul, killing his very own
Against the grain, to what was really home
Saved, after theology exposed him, lone
Who therefore is perfect?
Perfection not attained through research
No one trains, to become, perfect best !!!
By JESUS', Grace, others, accredited perfection
How, Jesusites, like, Abraham received adulations
Yes, how Heavenly angels acquire, congratulations
When Heavenly trumpets are sounding
Not all hearts are pounding
For not all, are facing hounding
Talking about Abraham, he was in the nineties
Did he have any friend of Heavenly quality?
He, therefore, like others, was a lone entity
Heavenly witness, on earthly own
The world denounced, only to bemoan
But, with Heaven, always feeling at home
The saints come together striking Heavenly accord
The kind of love, world can never afford
Unique cadence, guided by Heavenly cord
Something is Heavenly in the air
How many can see, to stare
Which hearts, pure enough to care
All, always, focusing on blessings
Without, in-depth understanding
Thinking, abundant wealth, they're receiving
Blessing, not about worldly wealth

No, not about financial health
Rather, Heavenly communion in-depth
Nothing about paper money
Making all behave very funny !!!
Pathetically, thinking, full up, in tummy

Blessing, having Heaven on your side
Ensuring, not fallen off the slides
Ordering your steps daily, without demise
We have no idea, what it feels like
To be fortunate enough to dive
Into the pool of Heavenly life
Something is hovering in the air indeed
Who has the spiritual eyes to see?
Who has enough in the heart to feel?
Some daring thing is hovering in the air indeed
Who has some goodness, to satisfy Heavenly needs?
Good enough with truthful deeds?
Heaven is hovering in the air, truth !!!
Who has the ability to really deduce?
Who is less worldly engaged to have a view?
For all are focused on telling gravely lies
To cover the worldly, wealthy trips, in miles
Believing, all about these smiles
Who has Heavenly angelic prominence?
Who values them in their physical presence?
We all, then, miss them, in their absence !!!
Who has Heavenly accepted elegance?
Coming before The Lord in confidence

Fruitfully yielding in Heavenly dominance
Want to meet one, with Heavenly prominence
With undoubted approved countenance
For, the harvest plenty, needs assistance
Who knows, we're not supposed to work !!!
No, never supposed to be engaged in dirt
Not to even wipe a sweat !!!
No one is supposed to work at all
But, receive Heavenly blessings and more
The kind, filling with Heavenly ore
We're not supposed to break sweat
Yet, never, to be in debt
Therefore, breaking boastings of worldly wealth
Working for anything we acquire is draining
Sinful slaves, thinking we're all brainy
Who has touch to live as such, bravely?
Religious teachings, empty rhetoric
Heaven detests tactical antics
We, so full of misleading heroics

WITNESS, REJECTED, LEAST, OR HIGHLY ELITE
FROM THE SERIOUSLY SKINT, TO FILTHY RICH
THE ADMITTED ATHEIST TO WORLDLY ANGEL
SHOULD DO SOMETHING, QUICK, ABOUT THIS
GETTING RID OF OUR EVERY DECEITFUL VIMS
AND EMBRACING SACREDLY, HEAVENLY WITS
UNPREDICTABLE TIMES RELIGIOUS LEADERS!!!
SHOULD ALL UNITE, AS HEAVENLY BROTHERS
TO ARREST, TRENDING, ATROCIOUS DANGERS

THROWING, INHERENT DIFFERENCES, APART!!
HUMBLY TO HEAVEN, INNOCENTLY, AS CHILD
AS ONE, ENGAGING, TO STOP, WORLD'S SLIDE
VENTURE TOWARDS, HEAVENLY PERFECTION
LIKE THESE HEAVEN'S ANGELS', ADULATIONS
IN ETERNAL, HEAVENLY, CONGRATULATIONS
SO PLEASE AWAKE, SPIRITUAL WORLD AWAKE

CHAPTER EIGHT

Religious Issues Regarding Paradise

I am nowhere near perfect!!!
Hence, of paradise, am I equally, bereft
Ensuring, vehemently, behind, sin, is left
But, religion doesn't know The Way!!!
Past events, they just replay
Thinking, this, Heaven says
Religion, ignorant of Heaven's redemptive Way
For, there exists only one, by the way
Who has the nous for Heavenly displays?
Religion doesn't know The JESUS Way
For, activities should be what Heaven says
Who has courage to be brave?
Religion is lost to The Way
For, housing, training, what, to it, relates
Only delivering what it conveys
Religion will never know The Way
As long as it assumes knowledge

For Heaven is approached with humble traits
Yes, religion, bereft of Heavenly countenance
Ignorant pride, evident dominance
Damaging temples in alarming circumstance

Yes, laying into, Heavenly appointed
Same, later acknowledging, Heavenly anointed
Religion, all, obviously, disjointed
Yet, Paradise is not lost
Those thinking they have, doesn't belong
But, those on whom, practically dawned
If Paradise lost, would be expensive cost
To the broken, humble heart, never, a loss
Compounding ignorant misery, not giving a toss
Paradise is for all, calling
Not of any use to the falling
But, deep thinker, from evil, stalling
Heavenly paradise, always for those
Humbly prepared to pose
In image of The Heavenly dose
Paradise remains for only those
Who, in Heaven's daily routine, poke the noses?
Not for the confused, in overdose
But, beautifully, accredited to those
Who have accepted The Heavenly notes
And their own songs to compose
Yes, dutifully belonging to homes
Who realize, that they are but, stones
Humbly, ready to be used as Heavenly domes

Readily reserved for, desiring those
Prepared to be turned from stones to gold
In best art gallery shows
Paradise, not for the spiritually cold
Or the assumed soon-to-die, old
But, those ready for Heaven, to rightly, scold
Everyone wants to be part of this Paradise
But who ably identifies One with the disguise
Leading to confirmed Heavenly compromise?
Blurry mind-set, attitude, means, difficult to identify
Apostles did it, hopefully, can humbly exemplify
Fairy tales can be real, this, would it, typify
Paradise belongs only to they,
Who realize that in whatever they do every day
Treat it like, their last day !!!
Will always be available for they,
Who The Lord's words they continually play
In their hearts, evidently, in their routine displays
Paradise will always be open for they
Who wash dirt in The Lord during the day
And with whom by night He comes to stay
Surely, forever belonging to they
Who are prepared to say
Enough, now, living The Heavenly Way

Paradise, if really is our desire,
Will seek The Heavenly roadmap required
Found fruitful, in His Distinguished repertoire
Seriously, if really, is our desire

Would cut off every indecisive wire
And reposition ourselves, in The Heavenly fire
Paradise, if truly, our desire
We'll burn off dazed worldly satire
And parade robes of Heavenly Polyester
Admittedly, will always be forever
For those, diligently warrant His pleasure
A way of life, in unimaginable flavour
We cannot pretend to have Paradise
He is not a state to jeopardise
Time, all religious leaders realized
Ready for homely Heavenly sealing of aperture?
Refurbished, ready with latest architecture?
Required, is the approval signature
It will be an undoubted travesty
If we don't turn around into Heavenly Dynasty
For, sufferings, require rest, in all honesty
Oh, what a disastrous travesty
If we don't leave this spiritual poverty
To avoid Heaven's ensuing penalty
Will not wish anyone to avoid Paradise
Therefore, do not wish that for ones
Who are, sadly, spiritually pale-wise

Success Interpretation

What, therefore, do we call success?
Is it what is a global business?
Or the executive power to overrule congress?
Winning millions of pounds in lottery?

Thinking there is no more misery?
Donating derisory farthings to some charity?
Highest formal educational accolade?
Inheriting relation's business empire for solace?
Which is nothing to the Heavenly mandate
All these, more, to Heaven, not success
For, not yielding personal divine progress
But, truthfully, some regrets and distress
Ministers, sinners, same target in success
Surely, doesn't make sense !!!
No wonder, all deeply distressed !!!
Ministers, criminals, chasing same success !!!
Who then are winners?
Heavenly lost souls under duress
Ministers, corporations, yearning equal reward
Who won't draw swords?
Strategic cost and fame at the fore !!!

Rinsing and drying blood out of the poor
Who physically evidently cannot afford
Then, thrown out of pathetic doors
Ministers, looters, seeking famous success
Heaven clearing all mess
Evident signs of worldly stress
What does the world call success?
Is it The Heavenly access?
Or what Heaven call dirt, we assess?
From His everlasting footstool
We make our deadly swoop
Thinking, we've so much scooped !!!

Sacredly Upholding Culture Consistently Eventually Secures Salvation
Nothing earthly, irrespective of qualification
But, everything Heavenly, to attain destination
Success, is reconnecting to The Creator
Absorbing prompts, living The will of The Mentor
To the delight of Heaven, The Master
If, this, our benchmark for success
We would better understand little stress
Laying foundations for others to climb upstairs
Heaven answers earthly telling questions
All situations sorted within few seconds
Ability within us, if we, Heavenly, make amends
We lack trust, in Heavenly pursuit
With wrong mind-set to achieve in truth
Our labouring, hew-and-cry, enough proof
All targeting over-ambitious targets
To show they are clever in buckets
All to gain what in the end has damaging regrets
Samuel, Paul, Israel, Jonah, Magdalene, encounter
When these ones spoke about The Alma mater
A reality the wise can't decipher
The educated can never discover
To the foolish, always a displeasure
But, to The Heavenly, the accepted barometer
Senseless, to human thinking !!!
Doesn't conform to worldly meaning
Paradiso, living without, sadly, a nothing thing
We need this life of austerity

We worry, sadly, called it severity
Yet, only saving grace, is Heavenly frugality

Serving Two Masters

For, no one serves two masters
One is sent to the sewers
The other uplifted to the rafters
No one can serve two masters
One seen among classy pillars
The other, among the homeless
None, really, serves two masters
One seen among innovators
The other, hopeless with beggars
Which is our master?
One ensuring we are richer?
Or one controlling our Heavenly stature
Which of them is our master?
The one providing, family, state-of-the-art villa?
Or One protecting from the evil doer?
Which of the two is our master?
The one who instigates disaster?
Or One strengthening for The Will of the Master?

JESUS is The One True Panacea
The Master qualified as Overseer
Before Him, there is none, a Seer

When child returns home with damaged fibula
Then hurting tibia, patella

Obviously, part of physical career
But when child returns with broken toe
Then, elbow and throat
Father knows it's HEAD-ING for his soul
Again, our current state
Which The Creator knows is not our place
So, serious work required to change fate
The Heavens aware of our goal
Not what we ably control
So ready for divine shoal
Religion has never been perfect
Preachers lying and lining pockets
Evidently, can never be, the Silver Bullet
Who wants to really "crack on"?
For, we should cease, being Heavenly phantom
To being bigger than an atom
Hence, we get spoken to, from which app?
The Heavenly one, ably beaming us up?
Or, one, that eternally, gets us clamped?
We get spoken to from which Adam's app better?
Is it modern day twitter?
Or through Heaven's humble individual router

Did the prophets carry any "books"?
No, they came as the news
What they brought, the learned can't diffuse
Their message that would explode
No hiding places, in any holes
For thieves have filled pockets and homes
The good news, they have refused

What they say, they worship, abused
Leaving The Heavens, not really bemused
No one wants to make the jump
Unto The Lord, for revamp
All have nothing, but the amp
Whose light shines in the night?
In the dark, there is no sight
Yet, His hands are opened with great might
Whose light remains shining in the night?
Who displays a well-drilled spiritual knight?
The devil, to defeat, in this fight?
Whose light keeps shining in the night?
For during the day, all looks bright
Should all start from the mind
Whose light shines in the dark?
When all seem to have hit a snag
Making it become, oh, so much stark
Who, of the repented, is a true star?
Before The Lord under true Heavenly VAR
Knowing that out of the devil, has come very far
Who, of the religious, is that one?
Who does The Lord's Will as He wants?
Not deceiving people with magic wand
Everyone wants to be seen
Not ashamed to hide terrible sins
Creating, rather, unrepentant scenes !!!
So, then, what is repentance?
Is it the thought, of God's acceptance?
Or, summary Heavenly renaissance?
Again, asking, what is repentance?

Confession of sins to some substance?
Or, renewal of shallow thoughts, for instance?
World, what is repentance?
Some worldly born-again stamps?
From someone who has no Heavenly stance?
What values so-called repentance?

Going to some pastor for deliverance?
Or, thought of Heavenly comitance?
What does world label repentance?
The total mind renewal after Heavenly stance
For, Heavenly Seal of Acceptance
Whoever acquires distinction, then, is distinct
Who bears that crown in the districts?
Who has Heavenly exemplary instincts?
To acquire distinction, be distinct
Also-runs, are not it !!!
Who has that extra bit?
Who desires being distinct?
Should cease from just existing
And, evil one, continually resist
Who is keen for Heavenly, distinct?
Should come out from being extinct
And into The Heavenly, insist
Who stands out distinct?
Preaching, praying, playing Martha, being strict
Or enjoying the free-for-all stint?
Who claims to be distinct
Let him, from evil life, desist
Characteristic of Heavenly eyes, succinct

Who, of the acclaimed is distinct?
Knowing The JESUS revealed disciplines
Acquiring The Heavenly approved distinction?
World, spends time, energy, resources to destroy
While peaceful dialogue, could deploy
Heavenly approved, brotherly ploy
When, against brothers, we lay deadly plots
Like loaded articulator over earthenware pot
Would be lucky, truly, to find a dot

WE SHOULD DAILY FIGHT TOOTH AND NAIL
ENSURING, WE'RE ON THE HEAVENLY TRAIL
SUCCESS INTERPRETATION HELPING US SAIL
NICODEMUS BUCKLED HAD TO DREAM REAL
STEPHEN, ANANIAS, AND OTHERS, YES, DEAL
HEAVEN'S REALM, NOW ETERNALLY SEALED
SERVING TWO MASTERS, HEAVENLY, INSANE
KEY COMPONENT, IN MISTAKES EACH MAKE
ACCEPTING, EVERYTHING IS VANITY, WASTE
ONENESS DESTRUCTION, THEN WITHDRAWN
HEAVENLY ONENESS MAKING ALL BLOSSOM
FOR IN HIM FIRMLY, GRACEFULLY, WINSOME
EACH ONE OF US SHOULD WAKE UP, WORLD

What is good, in being bad?
Like, nice, dead battery, without, spark !!!
When, world, does it ever start?
Where is joy, when mourning?
Not just about seeing next morning
But enjoying The Heavenly dawning

How are we divine in sin?
When we know, sin, we haven't binned
Achieving divinity, not, mere thing!!!

Religiously, No Remorse

Everyone is talking, no one listening
No one prepares for stalling
What happens when Heaven come calling?
Everyone, busily, fast talking
No one taking deep breaths, stopping
No wonder, we are all falling !!!
Everyone has legitimate opinion !!!
Wanting heads up, in the union
No wonder, no peace, in reunion
When illnesses cannot be diagnosed
Because of sinful overdose
Then, decaying carcasses, who has a nose?
The worldly thrills, one should miss
Onto the Heavenly, with Humble Kiss
Who have means, to make those kicks?
Yes, everyone wants to be seen
Including, breaking The Heavenly Seal
Destroying, approved, destined seed
So, we would have no ears to hear
Self-believing, we're already here
Who is going to dry every tear?
Hey, it would be, messy stage !!!
All one's life, with one message
Who, really then, is the sage?

This world, is in war zone
Who has strength to save his soul?
Who avoids this thick smoke?
The world, awoken, into war zone !!!
Casualties to take its toll !!!
Bringing to society, gaping hole !!!
World is facing, deadly war zone !!!
Catastrophic Armageddon on its own
But can stop evil world, not to fold

The world is besieged in a war zone !!!
Making all go 'wow no, wow'!!!
Yet, can love one another, so, won't roll
How good is worldly good?
When rooted in the evil's groove
Heavenly, zoomed, in doom
How good is our good?
When we can't win, will only lose
Yet, this evil, we choose
Making the value of our food
When we have all the clues
That to evil, we're all glued
Don't we know how bad our good is?
World requires a blitz
To correct, hits and misses
If we know how filthy we are, Heavenly
Would denounce everything openly
Desiring, new name, lovingly
Weighing the value of our good?
When The Heavenly food we refuse

Because we are set in our own views
How good is this earthly good?
Carrying Jekyll-and-Hide goods
With evil, thinking, Heaven, a fool
However, concerning Heaven, different terrain
Must be embedded in that domain
Only ENCOUNTER, is ordained
Religion, religion, religion, really legion
Making humanity lose positive reasoning
Ensuring, all cook with your tasty seasoning
"Thou shall not live by bread alone"
Yet, all we love, our selfish loaves
In any form, is all we toast
Thou shalt not live by bread alone
Yet, for us anything goes
So long as, wholly, in our bowls
"Actions speak louder than words"
What the world does worst
When it is to produce the best
Action speak louder than words
Preach gospel to uttermost parts of world
Imposter, blinded like earth worm
Action speak louder than words
No, not energetic, active, gestures
But fruit of seeds sown on divine pastures
Heaven does not desire vain words
Remember, His word landed in flesh
Those who actioned, He rightly blessed
Action speaks louder than words
Our actions reveal rotten dirt

Heaven wants one for clean-out first
For heaven has taken His aim
Who can stand without being maimed?
All like dried leaves, in the main
The Heavens has taken His aim !!!
Who will survive, including the dame?
Under what conceivable claim?
Yes, Heaven has positioned to aim
Who has strength to tame?
Avoiding everlasting wane

Innovating in Racism

Think to the depth of your skin
Your renowned next of kin
To whom you have become so akin
Think beyond skin colour
To smell the real friendly odour
Of the Heavenly artistic grandeur
Think beyond skin colour
And enjoy brother's culture
To make you even better
Let us think beyond skin colour
For we are all Heavenly matter
To daily help one another
World, please, move beyond skin colour
For healings faster than we'll ever consider
In our quest to meet The Master
Let's quickly move beyond skin colour
For, it's The Lord's marker

Of The Distinguished Creator
Again, should do better than skin colour
Should never deserve 'epicentre'
Of any comprehensive agenda
Time, spent on importance, not skin colour
For, Heavenly prospects, will shamefully hinder
Loving God without the brother, never!!!
Are green cars better than blue cars?
Insane question really, to ask someone?
Depicting, level of thinking, everyone
Downing values, talking daily, about colour
Are cars not judged by their quality rather?
Insane again, incensed, to, even bother
Should, rather, savour criticism
Sign of, possible, superior, interior mechanism
If indeed, really, worthy of any optimism

No one buys cars purely, by colour
Petty, therefore, dwelling on outer
One buys quality top of the Range Rover
We all dream, appreciate, Bentley
Value so much the Lamborghini
Or even the top German Mercedes
Who wouldn't want a Rolls Royce?
Full of its majestic poise
With all, exclusive, interior joys
So, why is world wasting time on colour?
My quality I daily master
Shows I'm best, no competitor
So, talk about my colour, appraises quality

No shame at all, being "blackie"
Why do "white" skins crave tanning?
Talk of outer, demonstrates inner quality
Yet, "black" skins desire lightening
Confused world, need Heavenly awakening
Life, not about colour outside
All about demonstrating Heaven with pride
For inside to gain eternity to reside
I am what I do, not skin colour
Without inner air, colour, non-starter
No wonder we're wasting away without an answer
Looking from Heavenly perspective, no anger
Filip to perform, even better
Obvious, therefore, definite no brainer
Should let go of racism nonsense!!!
Concentrating on our inner values instead
For, black and white, one day, would be dead
Let's grow up, loving one another indeed
Considering we're daily getting inter-married!!!
Enjoying time left before finally being buried
Racism, truly, glorified myth
Advertised, length, breadth and width
Serving others' profiles, hilarious whims
If once, was slave and master
If, in truth, slave, real bread winner
Better, dialogue, to resolve matter
No rights, wrongs, but foster
Worldly amicability, helping each other!!!
Remember, all rubbish, before Soul Provider
Never been about RACISM

But, depth of hatred's optimism
Destroying what is left of humanism
World gains, appreciating, everything made
Increasing, mind's healthy state
Connecting to all international states

Enriching, therefore, inner joy
Affecting others too, to rejoice
Bringing oneness, which all should deploy
From each home, to top, we make rules
Benefiting, only selected few
Exposing us, swimming in pool of fools
From "deprived, developed", all make rules
Issues, requiring few minutes to deduce
Take decades, centuries, to conclude
From deprived to developed, fashion rules
That, chosen few, only suits
Leaving rest, emotionally bemused
"Deprived," "developed", world over
Manufacture rules that homes, citizens, endanger
Straining heads around matter to another
Woe unto us tinniest to topmost rule makers!!!
Squeezing siblings, citizens, as wicked carers
Selves to blame, for worldly plunders
Disentangle, world, from meaningless mess
Wash selves clean, from this greed first
Before Heavenly link, consider, to assess
Refuse the present as nonsense, world
To plan how to Heavenly path, address
For time is ticking for untimely regrets

Every human has own world outside JESUS
Making decisions that oppose Heavenly features
Requiring a spin onto eternal ventures
All, are, individual rule-makers
Rubber-stamping what wicked minds tell us
Executing, what each assume, yields success
Seriously, world, in mishmash
Rollicking from pole to other, bashed
Would hurt now, but, for better Heavenly dash
For world, bad has become so good
Never only for those in the hood
Yeah, it has become being in the groove
Bad has become so sane
From it, all are slain
Who, has word, to say?
Abominations, things of the past
For, everyone, now, playing part
Approving abominable pacts
Bad, the norm, anything really goes
Dream woeful dream, would achieve goal
All do it differently, justifying growls
Yet, pulling hair out about others' roles
But, do worse, breaking Heavenly woes
Who holds back, in this sinful overdose?

Talking about grievous bodily harm
Some operate on the intestines
While others manage destructive minds
Living in age of lawlessness !!!
Doing what I want to do, regardless

Free world, no one renders me speechless!!!
Congregations becoming united
Do we want to be invited?
Majority are already suited
Religion, truly, merging
But, really, Heaven, searching
Seeking where all leading
These are emphatically, no dreams!!!
Certainly not like eating ice-creams
Involving hard work and screams
These are obviously no dreams!!!
Not like crossing tiny streams
Entailing lots of hard-core freaks
No, desirably, not dreams!!!
Full of frightening creaks
Surely, not like eating breams!!!
Verily, verily, all in haste
Delicious foods always to taste
No, no time to delay, nothing to waste
Yes, everyone, verily in haste
Spreading deliciousness of its fate
All are eating, so nothing, out of date
Oh, how good, who is the cook?
Really, well done, from which book?
Will always be sitting on this wood
This is yummy, who is the cook?
Would recommend it, very good
For me, best food…

"World should not live by bread alone"
"Rather, every world out of The lord of Hosts"
Only this FOOD, makes us whole
The Holy Books, rightly, for reference
Not dictating, how, I, Heaven, today reverence
Hence, The Lord's word, daily, my preference
Heaven's fresh word, food for soul
Never found in just, any bowl
Exclusive, from source, sacredly honed
Only JESUS provides, Him, alone
ALL souls humbly seeking His road
He freely gives, directing prodigal son home

EVERYONE BELIEVES, HEAVENLY, A CONSTANT
RELIGIOUS EN-ROUTE, NO REMORSE, ADAMANT
NEVER, WERE TWO MASTERS, NO GRANDSTAND
HENCE, EMULATING HUMBLE ANGELICS AGAIN
ATTITUDE, BEFITTING NAMES WE HAVE TAKEN
HEAVEN ENDORSING, PERFECT ONES IN PLACE
ERADICATING, DREADFUL INNOVATIVE RACISM
FOR, HEAVENLY ONENESS, MAKES US, BLOSSOM
SO, IN HIM BECOMING INEXPLICABLY WINSOME
THUS, LET US ALL AWAKE, WAKE UP, OH WORLD

The Heavenly journey, not plain sailing
We've been swayed, can only be wailing
The wrong heaven, we are hailing
Get off quickly, off the railings
To all others, we should be mailing

For, still chance for bailing
All have fallen, facing, jailing
None the least aware, we are failing
Never the promised head, we are tailing
Everyone, now devouring vulture
The congregation he would daily torture
Oh Lord, wherein, the future?
Yes, everyone, full blown vulture
Killing every son and daughter
Including one calling himself, doctor
The world is led to the slaughter
Hell fire will start to smoulder
Oh, who to save, where, the mother?
World chained, bound for slaughtering
Blazing fire, set, already destroying
Who stops this to start fostering?
World, helpless, from where we lie
Completely overcome, being tied
No hope, just about getting ready to die
Oh, if someone could just pass by
Like JESUS, saving us from someone's pie
Yes, offer some money for us to buy
Who will save, and quickly before sunrise?
Who has strength, for all to arise?
To then, eventually, heave, relieved sigh
Heaven gave us His all
Yet, greedily, demanded more
But, Heaven did not say, done enough
Heaven gave us everything

We thought we knew something
Without Heavenly intervention, have nothing !!!

Heaven provides everything needed
Yet, for more, we constantly pleaded
We've lost all, we yielded !!!
We thought we're smarter than maker
Thinking, too slow, He is a faker
Slowly working, as The Baker !!!
Instead of God, machines talk to us
Hence, instead of growing, we gain less
Thinking we've gained, we're penniless
Hence, religion needs to find The Way
But not with, dreadful array
Of obvious disillusioned disdain
But, who will know, who will believe?
So consumed, in what's conceived
Displaying noisily, vanity, achieved
Who said JESUS turned water into wine?
That is truly fine
But, NEVER a physical sign !!!
Yes, JESUS did turn water into wine
But, was demonstrating Heavenly line
Only acquired with defined attitudinal kind
Yes, He did turn water into wine
But not what has served the pastors' time
For not letting go, to receive Divine Vine
By His Grace, I breathe, JESUS turned water into wine
Not the notorious pastors and reverends jibe

That has got the whole world confused till now
We've all shot ourselves in the foot !!!
Taken a whack from the boot
Opening the way, for pathetic loot
We've all shot ourselves in the foot !!!
For, so wrongly, we recruit
Yeah, from root to fruit
Still, shoot ourselves in the foot !!!
For, all deeds, mere soot
With what then, do we now soothe?
We've really shot ourselves in the foot !!!
Like laboured lone horse without hoof
What is the essence of a roof !!!
Who is ready to replace the tooth !!!
Rendered helpless, can only, but hoot
Who to save, who to us, cool'?
All hooting remains a mime
No remedy, with a heavy fine
On our side, is no time
Not believing, religious merger, not strong !!!
Not wanting change, old ways to always throng
Hanging on, to old religion, Heavenly wrong

Who does not believe religion merger?
Assuming that would spell bad weather
JESUS declares, loving one another
Thinking, will never happen in lifetimes
Others assume, will be a long while

So, should keep up fun and smiles
Assuredly, these are no lies
Love God, love one you see with eyes
Refusing this, being as cold as ice
Who is our enemy, when we, do not love?
It is the only one person we show we have
He knows when it is easy for us or tough
The world, advancing in its innovation
Heaven is way improving His destinations
Upgrading rejected, unskilled, in His organisation
When we don't like our place
We end up with what we hate
For losing track of our taste
Disliking, hard-worked-for, place
End up with pathetic date
Then, treated as food thrown out of plate
Sadly, again, world's unenvious state
From top to bottom cannot contemplate
What future, world, at stake?
For, Heaven doesn't need gloves, to, us, pummel
Seeing we're nowhere near Heaven's peripherals
Following evil father's, principles
Vain, weak, empty, pathetic mortals
labelled with decayed foundational
In trajectory, only eternally fatal
All about world, deeply, simply, suicidal
Without, slightest breath of survival
Only Mad, Spirit Man, invokes, upheaval

The Spiritual Mad Man

Who is the spirit man?
Who makes the world think he is bad?
Because, it thinks he is mad
A mad man, who does he not like?
In him there is no spite
To see another day, he is fine
This man competes with who?
To him everything is new
He simply has no clue
Truthfully, minding his own business
Who would give him good reference?
He just has no preference
Mad man, therefore, lives on rejected
Selects what is left of neglected
Making friends with who he selected
Gathers, what is left, with him, he surrounds
The weight, carrying them around
And, we wonder, what all that is about?
How long does he live before death?
Eating from what we call dirt
Where did it go wrong, after birth?
This is how Heaven sees us, so-called rich
Collecting, gathering, amassing, then, ditched
Living as though, forever, around, stick
Finding out, next second, we're gone
Memory of same madness, longed for
Pathetic cycle, should readily be stopped

The mad man is friends with everyone
But, who wants to be close to THIS MAN?
He rarely has company in this land
The mad man wishes to be friends with everyone
So, anything he finds, he has won
Who wants to stay with that one?
For, there is a strange MAD MAN
Sees everything whole, He does man
So, then, before Him, who is the man?
Competing with no one in this world !!!
In different league, living so well
In The Heavens, He is more than His worth?
Ignored by all, thinking we are big !!!
But, our own holes, we daily dig !!!
Who to save, from this pit?
The MAD MAN, seen as not there !!!
But, who in reality, has gone where?
How well does anyone fare?
Concerning this MAN, wo knows better?
In search of subsistence, we always batter
Which, to Him, not even mere bread and butter
He makes our knowledge, useless !!!
Being haughty, thinking, fullness !!!
Yet, presumed astute in business !!!
Busy, really for what is decayed !!!
Craving what MAD MAN relays !!!
Without access, for, from Him, we refrain !!!
Yes, Heavenly MAD ONES have no friends
So, stones, decay they pick and mend
Ready for whose ears, are lent

Apostles took a chance with Him
When all thought His light was dim
With Him, nothing good to win
Hypocrites, His birthday not for celebration

Death, also, time for stock, serious deliberations
For woeful, fatal accusations
We celebrate His death and resurrection
As though we did not demand His execution
Shameful, for not even disguising decisions
Don't even know exact spot, laid
What do we care now, after Him, we slay?
His birth, death, do we really know dates?
Awake, world for getting it all wrong
Created everything, being false
Obliged to this, other holes, initially plug
This rewinding, others, should accelerate
To reverse consequence onto us, deliberate
For our souls, to sacredly fumigate
Before, ourselves, we do more damage
Worsening the already unscrupulous carnage
Where are so-called KNOWLEDGABLES?
Who are so-called ASTROLOGISTS?
All are copying and pasting, failing in plagiarism !!!
Angels like Noah, dwelt among us with the news !!!
Feeding from on high, with Heavenly view
Accordingly, tells world, how to get a clue !!!
Lacking respect, worries, identifying Him
He comes across, unimpressively, ordinary
Disguised blueprint, foolish pride falls victim

Vital, raising respectability levels
Lead us through troubled tunnels
Humility required, crucially, vital
Should one appear anywhere, everywhere, world
We need in-tuned, epic spirituality here
Overcoming static friction, will lead us there
The Mediator, Saviour, JESUS The CHRIST
In Him, no known cries
Freely giving to who just thinks and tries
Who is who before Him?
Even when singing Him a hymn
His words, give meaning and whim
Oh, that I can do His will !!!
That I can truly worship Him !!!
For, His money I always steal from His till
Oh that I can find Him
And tell Him what I think
To allow me, Heavenly wink
What happens to our desire?
When He only wants willing warrior?

Would pause, acknowledge effort, as character !!!
If His calls we could respectfully hear on phones
But definitely, not deadly, worldly tone
From His Unimaginably Heavenly Throne !!!
Surely, at best, world, puts us on hold
Should believe Him, being bold !!!
Reaching for worldly untold
Apostles met a VAGABOND, whole !!!
Most talked-about, JESUS, of old !!!

Only One, accustomed to Heaven's Road !!!
We are grateful, Sir JESUS
For fighting hard to redeem us
Especially, me, the worst of sinners !!!
Yes, only You know, right, for us
We will stride with bold hearts !!!
Focusing on YOU to successful heights
Best music, anyone would hear
Knowing, beginning of end, here !!!
For complete salvation, so, very near
Ensuring, no more, will there be, a tear

ENCOUNTER, WITH HEAVEN'S MAN, SURREAL
SHOULD HUMBLY FIND HIM TO SECURE DEAL
FEEDING ALL, DESPITE COVID, DEAL TO SEAL
WE ALL, NEED TO BECOME CHILDREN, AGAIN
OUR ANSWER TO, TRENDING HEAVEN'S RAGE
CEMENTING THE ETERNAL HEAVENLY PLACE
PIVOTAL, MAKING HEAVENLY TELLING MOVE
THUS, IN HIM BECOMING SACREDLY WINSOME
TIME, AWAKE, HENCE FROM SLUMBER, WORLD
FROM THE LEAST TO THE ELITE
THE SKINT TO THE FILTHY RICH
ATHEIST, TO, EARTHLY ANGELS
SHOWING HUMILITY, ABOUT, IT
RIDDING, OF UNWANTED, VIMS
IDENTIFYING, HEAVENLY- WITS
SO, AWAKE, UP, OH, YES, WORLD

CHAPTER NINE

What Heaven Does

When Heaven touches and teaches you
Like apostles, creates you anew
To confound those who said they knew
When Heaven handpicks and reconciles with you
He continues His eternal rescue
Developing you, in Him, to stay renewed
When The Heavens call and teach recovery
Not about stopping smoking, drinking, adultery
Nor prostitution, stealing, lying, idolatry
When The Heavens reveals Himself
Nothing concerning worldly respect
Nor the carnal traditional concepts
With The Heavens yelling your time
Forget your riches or pathetic dime
You'll be purified like with lime
Yes, when Heaven yells that it's your time
You will run from all with whom you dine
Till as He likes it, the world sees you shine
But, like Job, with no worldly friends

To them, you're now mad needing a mend
All the big boys followed same trend

Salvation

The message of salvation
Who knows His station?
To acknowledge His destination?
No one has ever seen The Christ !!!
The One who did arise
To tell His real Price
The message of salvation, so sweet
Not preached in the streets
As religion uses it for riches at speed!!!
Remember, JESUS, because of salvation value
Takes apostles out of public view
And gives them, Sacredly, what is their due
No one has ever seen The Christ
The One who will strike !!!
Because of the waste, regarding His stripes
Has anyone ever seen The Christ?
The authority that ushers the weak to rise
To receive, from Him, the valued Prize
The sacred message of salvation
Who justifies it by intuition?
To request people pay at institutions
He is never required by inclination
With world deceived through desperation
Or conjured via some incantations
The Heavenly salvation supplication

How do we give Him valuation?
To make people pay donations
This humbling message of salvation
Has His own station in a station
And His own destination in a destination
The sought-after message of Salvation
Will never be known by Archimedes' calculations
Or determined by mediums' divinations
This Heavenly message of salvation
Not just for any impaired vision
Or those of any kind of physical restrictions
This everlasting message of salvation
Does not belong to those facing destitutions
Or those very rich beyond description
Yes, the precious message of salvation
For those who belong to the Heavenly nation
Proving their worth, by their daily notions
This long-awaited message of salvation
Truly, has specific operation
Not defined by scientific experimentations

Who then knows about salvation?
When all are loving worldly presentations?
Milking in so-called innovations
Hence, what is priceless salvation
Who has marks for His qualification?
Definitely not entire population !!!
Never, the physically obvious
Who think they are so pious
In people's eyes, so precious

Belongs to these who ceaselessly long!!!
From creation of the world and beyond
Sniffing and living as such, oh so long
Salvation is a different matter
Not belonging to religious leaders' splutter
Entails interest from every sector
Salvation has unique chapters
Not belonging to one who flatters
But, take account of jittering grafters
Salvation, always a serious subject
Not belonging to the abject
But, who sees Him as more than an object
Salvation is in different stratospheres
Far above our atmospheres
Not for mingling around these hemispheres
The angels who land from the skies
Come in heavy disguise
To identify them, requires Heavenly eyes
The angels, sent from the skies
Reflect as one of the guys
But never of worldly styles
These angels dropped from the skies
Operate with so much guise
Definitely, not human spies
Those angels who descend from the skies
May have the same jersey in stripes
But, wearing Heavenly spikes
With them, "Holy Books" are re-written
New material matching new printing

For a people, with renewed thinking
The "Holy Books" are being re-written
For people with Heavenly innovative feeling
Upholding The Most High, way above the ceiling
The "Holy Books" have a reviewed scope !!!
For all who dared, and gladly have a home
A great reward, for who manages to cope

Yes, the "Holy Books" have renewed dimensions
Farther afield, with expensive extensions
Who won't want to partake of these diversions?
The "Holy Books" are already here !!!
To ensure no one has a tear!!!
Everyone who did all, to adhere !!!
The "Holy Books" have always been among us
For The Creator has opened the prospectus
And has among us, special inspectors
Doing what is, normal daily duties
But relaying and receiving Heavenly goodies
Goodies, only to one ready and receives
The "Holy Books" never lie !!!
Readily available for who wants to stay alive
Without which, all will surely, wastefully, die !!!
Guess what, these "Holy Books" won't be for sale
Without them, can only grow pale
For every food, would then, be stale
These "Holy Books" are unique !!!
They live in the hearts of the Lord's indeed
Every soul that needs food, fed as a unit

They define the messengers
As what we should be, not religious leaders
Exemplary examples for us as harbingers

When Heaven at the Fore

When Heaven is at the fore
There is a designed Protocol
That is well and truly assured
When organised Heaven is at the fore
We're connected by His Umbilical Cord
So, to Him, we're indefinitely joined
Yes, having the Heavens at the fore
Means, at last we'll be one, of course
What our various religions couldn't restore
Graciously, Heaven being at the fore
We strike a co-ordinated chord
Which is very uncommon
When unusual Heaven is at the fore
We do not know about being bored
For we continually receive and more
Ah, Omnipresent Heaven at the fore
We are never sore!!!
For His goods, we are core !!!
Yes, when Heavenly operations are at the fore
For us, an easy war
For He does not even need to roar !!!

Truly, guiding Heaven at the fore
We are controlled by His cord

Directed by The Rod
With Gracious Heavens at the fore
We are always informed
Leading us inside, beyond, our door
When mercifully, Heaven is at the fore
Each receives due call
Duties to perform in tip top form
Powerful Heavens at the fore
Into the devil He dutifully tore
With His ever sharpened exclusive paw
Gigantic Heaven is at the fore
Grabbing the bull by the horns
So, we go through bushes without a thorn !!!
I'll prefer The Heavens at the fore
For what we call unrelenting chore
Is like enjoying the beach's sun at shore
When The Heavens is yours at the fore
There is legitimate hoard
Filling barns and stores
Beaming The Heavens at the fore
Every impediment, He gladly floors
With His distinctive, custom-made claws
Yes, The Heavens will always be at the fore
To His angelic beloved, every good, pour
As the priceless, distinguished ore
Dare I say, sacredly, rich Heaven at the fore
He gives to all, and whatever we wore
Who wants to know HE is LORD?
None better than Captain Heaven at the fore
Navigating, sent angels, always, to superbly perform

Expressing joy beyond awe !!!
When reliable Heaven at the fore
Readily available to those He is for
To others, mysterious metaphor
So, why shouldn't we install Him to our fore
Stopping, operating with the devil as whores
To be first to respond when He calls !!!
When Omnipresent Heaven is at the fore
He prepares everything for believers, prior
Tracing our way through, only to soar
So, when protecting Heaven is at the fore
Like Jonah, you are excellently secure
For no intelligence is on call
Evidently, when The Heavens rally at the fore
He pre-empts above all
Providing abundantly and beyond

This is why Heaven will always be at the fore
Unlike doctors, no life is lost
Everyone, important, and ably reforms
We would love having Heaven at the fore
Knowing that there is no con
With abundant, lifetime, holiday resort
Who wouldn't want The Heavens at the fore?
Knowing, in everything, you would outscore
For being in The Eternal Hardcore
We thank The Heavens for being at the fore
Acknowledging that we would enjoy forevermore
In line with every belief and folklore

Cannot wait, therefore, for Messiah's return
Occasion, most are keen to envisage this term
His coming nigh, some pretty firm
Never been easy, having Heaven at the fore
Knowing only lifestyles, uncalled-for
To believe, on Heavenly concord
When, own pastors think we are evil
For smelling threats to dubious principles
Chasing you, dead, compounds own peril
Ask JESUS about dangerously, sad ordeal
Saying, He is The Real Deal
Pastor's misdeeds, He knows, to reveal?
No way, Jose, won't live to tell a tale
Blasphemous, nincompoop, nay!!!
Thinking, "I've nurtured you to be somebody today"
Great, having Heaven at the fore judiciously
Better regimented than any military, religiously
Armament intelligence, unifies, constructively

HEAVEN'S LOST SHEEP, SALVATION, REAL
HUMBLE HEARTS, ENSURE, ANGELIC SEAL
HEAVEN AT THE FORE, THEN, ARE DEALS
SALVATION, RECEIPT, ESSENTIAL MATTER
HEAVEN AT THE FORE, RELAYS PLEASURE
LIVING WITH HEAVENLY ICONS, FOREVER
SO, AWAKE, WAKE UP WORLD, ITS DOABLE
QUICK, WORLD, FASTER, ON THE DOUBLE!!
MESSIAH, ALWAYS MAKES THIS, A DODDLE

Messiah Coming Nigh

My lucky charm is this wood,
Was not enjoying where I stood
Have, surely found myself, very good stool
Now, can afford, enjoying bowling
No hard labour, regarding towing
In Heavenly joy, I am sowing
The end, according to Heaven, nigh !!!
Accredited, readying for cloud nine
Any chosen, left behind, none
The end accordingly is nigh !!!
Everyone heading for the Nile
Trying hard, off, messy pile
The end is surely nigh !!!
Who chooses, calls it a lie
But worthless death, won't want to die
Heaven's announcing, end, surely nigh
Interested, should be now
Before, regretfully, aside, to go, wow!!!
Heaven calls, world, at its end
None, anything, here and now, mend
Without JESUS, nothing has Heavenly scent!!!
Inevitable end, definitely nigh !!!
From evil, should cut ties
Into Heavenly bosom, lie
Not alone, narrating, end, nigh
Hence, surely, no more time
No longer, about what we like

End time approaching, very nigh
Not time, explaining why
But feeling, in spine
Not as expected, but end, definitely nigh
Exiting rubble, should, climb high
Avoid, devouring fire
Yes, end time, readily nigh
No longer on mount Sinai
But in hearts, Heavenly financed
Heaven asserts, the home stretch !!!
Encouraging, re-fillings, fetched
Renewing confidence for the end, be fresh
Heaven asserts, home stretch !!!
Into Heavenly values, drenched
On fences, can none perch !!!
Heaven calls about home stretch
Like five foolish, no regrets
Empowered anew, shall we be sketched
Envisaging, clinching fists
For accredited rewards, that fit
Joy untold, would be in bits
Hard work, nearing a close
Difficulty ahead, some easily froze
But, readily negotiating meandering roads

We expected, would be difficult!!!
With strong legs and control, none, to somersault
The Heavens at the helm, none out of sorts
Yes, end fast approaching !!!

Never, time for coaxing!!!
Fired up for battle, within, roasting !!!
The Heavens confirms "Finish Hard" !!!
Finish hard the town cry, no more time to retard
Retarding a-plenty, later, not time to hamper!!!
The end is nigh, Heavenly cry
Above call, we time to pry
Leaving all empty, high and dry
World, oblivious to this cry !!!
Expecting rains at dry times
Only Heaven, scores this try
So-called religious, talk, end times
Still, wasted energies, and at primes
Least aware, visiting, deadly shrines
Heaven finds funny, religious teachings
Conveyed as, "rain is shining"
Hilariously, "sun is raining"
For activities scream without clue
They, and all crew
For, all engagement, cruel
Not every hole, a pocket !!!
Nor all holes, fit all sockets
Quickly, shoot evil hole, as rocket
Not every hole ends hollow
From Heaven, none want to fall low
Imperative, Heaven, we follow
With The Heavens, there is no sorrow
Important team member, a fellow
Hearts, yelling HELLO, each feels and knows !!!!
Everyone desires peaceful home

Calling, his very own
Welcoming place for soul
With Heaven, positive motive
Knowing He is the Positive
Bad, I'm the negative
Saying, like poles retract
Assuredly, opposites attract
Humble one has a contract
One of reasons, Heaven quakes !!!
What He has, no one, nothing takes
Heaven, definitely, not fake !!!
Suffering for the repented sake
Sweeping negativity in His wake
To bake best cakes

The Heavens, not easy to find
Not type in carnal minds
Identification, difficult kind
He is ready for confessions
From sinners, all profession
We've all joined the procession!!!
Procession identifying Heavenly limitations
Limitation not auguring well, worldly aspirations
Aspiration, fading fast with failed expectations
Expectation, dissolved in deceptions
Deceptive wasted efforts, on reflection
Wouldn't have known without intervention
Interventions, through communication
Communications borne out of frustrations
Frustration remits determination,

The determination, bolstering dissemination
This dissemination breeds revelation!!!
Revelations into Heavenly reconciliation
That, spiritual emancipation yields redemption
The Heavenly kind, without oppression
From The Ultimate's sacred resurrection
For, all we've done, sinister
There is none, a minister
For none answered calls from register !!!
Should learn from initial Adam
Also, Isaac's, involving Abraham
Heaven wants clean hearts not just enjoying ham
Singing "Lord I Lift Your Name On High"
Doesn't get to Him any nigh
Thinking we've performed with sighs
He doesn't listen to our sweetest songs
Our mouths, hearts, same, does not belong
For, with the devil, have we become fond
When someone comes from somewhere
To narrate what's there
You either believe or dare !!!
Heavenly road, no one able to teach
Whose roses haven't we peached?
For, nothing like going to the beach
All profess, ability to teach
Self-styled doctrines, they only preach
For Heaven, away from the lot, I Beseech
All acclaim Heaven they teach
Yet, every move, they ignorantly breach

Onto Heavenly gas, should they screech
All clamour for huge congregations
Thinking Heavenly ordained, total degradation
Sadly, succeeding in segregation

Maybe truly repeating self
Because, doom is set, really hurts
Lying to those needing help
Finally, time to tell
When people escape this spell
The Lord's, congruently, doing well
Team bonds good blend
Even with taste bland
Nothing like Heavenly Brand !!!
Deceitful commander, very smooth
To tactically train in his school
Why, Heavenly ones can't feed, no spoon!!!
We've no life here, without controversy
Why we continually seek His Mercy
Realizing we're all very messy
Accepting, we have a long way to go
To where the biggies call home
Not yet achieved distinguished goal
To the Heavens, we should be viscous
Avoiding anything that causes discourse
For in Him is all the resource
Laying down outweighing burdens
Individually, daily, communicating with Heaven
Treading on road where bread is leavened

Human Temple Change Needed

Disliking Heavenly association
Hungers into threatening situations
Ending in abominable destinations
Focus not on evil controlling, not time
For, he hasn't, dime
Rather on Messiah, Paradise in sight
Where are the ministers?
Again, supposed leaders
What is happening to followers?
Who are the ministers?
Supposed frontrunners
What's happened to worshippers?
You, calling yourselves ministers
Supposed pace setters
Where are your educated?
Claimants, as ministers
Therefore serial forecasters
Wherefore your trailers?
Who are the ministers?
With The Heavenly Imperial Sceptre
Displaying not being modern day satyr
Deserting, place for the living
Deadly terrains chosen for live-in
Oh, how The Heavens is livid !!!
Lightening up streets with distinctive eyebrows
Admirers cheering names with prowls
Flaunting shining beautiful crowns

You're pathetically toothless
Your controller always ruthless
Leaving you, completely clueless
You who control ministers
Therefore seasoned instructors
Wherefore your innovators?
Who heads these ministers?
Supposedly, taking ones out of gutters !!!
Now, worse than gangsters!!!
Oh, if there was a crystal ball
For all to pre-see the greatest fall
Would then know about heeding Heavenly call
Toddler, I wave to every passer-by
Most smile, without asking why
So, why, now, change for worse, with time?
All the "Holy Books" are good
But if the cook doesn't follow the rule book
He doesn't get the right food
It is okay having the "Holy Books"
You cannot bake cake without following rules
Holding "Holy Books", not doing what's due
Building, if plan, messed up
Will not be able to stand !!!
Everything falls apart
Same, Heavenly levels, not reached !!!
Sin, pray for forgiveness, growth we breach
Marking time, attempting, erasing sin with bleach !!!
Consequently, instead of progress
We've sadly retrogressed

Transgress, brag, transgress
Never time, despising others, about JESUS !!!
Nor comparisons with Mohammed
Time, to seek individual, Heavenly heads
Not to expect MESSIAH
Nor yelling, Allah
But, find, Heavenly, where, each are !!!
Prayers heard, hope, onto which we cling
Hate and hope, vice-versa, not Heavenly thing
Yet, very rubric of our being !!!
Our gospels, not Heavenly accepted
The orchestra we've always conducted
Passionate words, not heart orchestrated !!!
Being furious about corrections
Yet, presumably, seek perfection
Obstinate student, left at own discretion !!!
No one succeeds without, leader
No one peaks without, trainer
JESUS, listens to Father !!!

"Holy Books", contaminated, by evil nature
Therefore, needing, Heavenly stature
Whose knowhow revamps stable nurture?
We've condemned "Holy Books" with actions
On us, therefore, are Heavenly sanctions
For HUMBLE, positive reaction !!!
What we think we have, we've destroyed !!!
For no one, by the tactics, deployed
Heaven, not deceived by hypocritical ploys
It's all about re-awakening !!!

HUMBLE, to accept re-positioning
Readied heart, for new beginning
All should divert course
With massive chunk of remorse
For joyous Heavenly concords
We were not created to work
If in doubt, ask a bird
Adam told them what he heard
What can we really boast of?
Breathing improperly, when oxygen not enough
Control own blood-flow, we cannot !!!
HUMBLE mind-set claims nothing !!!
Child, not needing anything
Another day, enough, everything
What therefore, do we have?
Don't own a hair, for a start
Begin with HUMBLE heart
Should seek Heavenly innovation
Before considering earthly elevations
But who catapults onto Heavenly aviation
Recognise each, important
Priority, not, popular stunt
Becoming, Heavenly redundant
Nurture **E**veryone **E**specially **D**utifully
Global family, displayed daily, beautifully
Joy abounding as kids, bountifully
We **A**ll **N**eed **T**ogetherness !!!
Imperative, we encourage ONENESS !!!
Divisions, sadly, breed lawlessness !!!
No wagering requirements, leaders impose

Should humbly educate to eventually riposte
From Heavenly truth, this, evidently remote
See each as God, passionately, we love
We'll live in truth, as done above
Then, rightly called, beloved
Racism, a thing of the past
Seeing each, as you, a must !!!
News of joy, everywhere, very fast !!!

From home to streets
Nice to every one we meet
Beginnings, of sorting own needs
In cab, driver, family, vice-versa
Not contemplating discount, runner
Culture, resonating with Heavenly member
No longer propounding theories !!!
But, good, spiritual stories
Should create own Heavenly histories
We don't need temporary heroes
But each caring, like foods in silos
When required, abundant in kilos
When all, nice to all
Costs generally fall
National defence expense tumbles !!!
Overall health improves
Mental health issues to nought, reduce
From all sorts, youth, rescued
Blood pressures, become normal
NHS operations nicely optimal
Targets, no longer suicidal

Then, to "Holy Books"
To enjoy the word, divine food
That Heaven, for each, always cooked
Brains, understanding better
Completely new letter
To enjoy lives better, this latter
Feel, turns, humbly new
The kind, enjoyed by Holy few
Bankrolled to all, saying, phew
From me, for those around
To know exactly what I'm talking about
May sound like boxing bout
Requires change in mental faculty
To enter Heaven, which is reality
We all, atheism, vanished from society
So-called religious, now walk the talk !!!
Seeing, no longer false
Impact, means, another joins walk !!!
Responsibility to make lives easier !!!
Demonstrating lifestyles as Heavenly leader
For all to become, brother and sister !!!
No longer, talking differences in religion
Back to the beginning
Each, a RELIGION, demonstrates true living !!!
Talking ONENESS, not religion !!!
That carried unnecessary segregation
But, to yield, Heavenly inspiration

We, individually are, religion, we profess !!!
My religion, my walk, will confess

Faith without works, only transgress
Enough, with hatred !!!
Cannot hate and stay sacred
Lies, rooted in hades !!!
Enough hate!!!
Let's destroy envy
To realize, we're ready
Enough blackmail
Going for all male and female
Let's jump onto Heavenly trail
Exemplified as toddlers, better, as adults
Let's dutifully turn back clocks
Putting evil in gridlock
Lives having suffered, including Brexit
Helter-skelter, without entrance or exit
Monies could 've been of better benefit
Controls costing money
Look back, thinking, it's funny
Very unnecessary, when all, sunny
Again, starting from me
An example we all need
Let's start, gather speed
Time, not on world's side
But, can surely change tide
When we take positive strides
All about examples
My positive Heavenly sample
Which the human God finds ample
We did it while young
Let's pick it up, having been stung

With poison through our lungs
We can stop it, when we try
Did it when young, should not be shy
To score Heavenly TRY !!!
The ball, in our court
Should be bold, taking the fort
Getting stronger, going along
Religion should let another knock on my door
Saying, I see you in daily awe
I want to know why, and more
Another should knock on my door
Then follow, to hear more
So, eventually, no more war
Religion should let another knock on my door
Confidently say, now, no war,
Demonstrating, what's there for all

When talking of knock on doors
Not mere door, but heart, welcoming, warm
Relating to all, as twins, quality ores
Religion should let another see me and say
I do not know what you do every day
But, one thing for sure, I want to know your way
Should let me be an example
For another, to Heavenly tremble
Pursuing Eternal samples
My personal religion should entice another
A wrong-doing one to surrender
For, the much craved, hereafter
My demonstrated religion should let another confess

Not by mouth, but, by deeds, to digress
For his benefit, family in Heavenly success
Yes, I should allow my religion to demonstrate
How to, worldly unnecessities, confiscate
For the benefit of The Heavenly escapade
Truly, religion should let one in the community
Be positive example in society
Affecting more, in positivity
Yes, personal religion should influence
People, of all cultures in congruence
As, state-of-the-art attitudinal reference
Personal religion should show behaviour
That all should daily, endeavour, to conquer
And others, portrayed daily from reservoir
My religious influence should put my arms
Around another of another religion without qualms
Eating from same bowl with "clean hands"
Causing a stir, regionally
Quickly extending, nationally
Innovation advent, spreading, globally
The five foolish women
Is it because they woo men?
Or they would not mend
Those five foolish women
Because they won't blend?
Or they wouldn't learn
Either way, unable to demonstrate
No, couldn't embrace
Their titles, they couldn't reciprocate!!!

Change School and Meals

Hence, not the titles, we call ourselves
Never what we think we deserve…
But truly, what we have in reserves
If mathematician cannot calculate 10x1
Opposes being fired, what does he want?
Does he qualify for what he says to have?
Fisherman knowing nothing about nets
Saying fish are caught in "nests"
What will he do next?
Baker knowing nothing about flour
What's he going to do with a flower?
How does he use a plier?
Supermodel, never heard of catwalk
And says she hasn't a cat, to walk
Takes everyone for a mug
Pilot, doesn't know about cockpit!!!
Englishman, doesn't understand, sit
Smoker, doesn't know how cigarette is lit !!!
Nicodemus and, "born again" example, gross !!!
This is how bad, it is a loss
For one who called himself, spiritual BOSS !!!
A complete waste of resource !!!
All those years of inclusion without tapping source
Oh no, master-chef never heard of oxo sauce
What has been my responsibility ?
What did I call my ability ?
What therefore, again, my accountability ?
When a pastor, a blatant liar
A doctor never heard of exercising CPR
You surely wouldn't know where you are !!!

This is who we all are, in the eyes of the Lord !!!
Who thinks I am wrong?
Show, Heavenly, what you have worked for?
The Heavenly roadmap like a school
Head of school, sets the rules
For all to obey to stay put
The Heavenly focus, like a school
Chief examiner determines, all use correct tools
So, in the end won't be fools
The Heavenly trail, likened to a school
Each name inscribed, according to equipment use
So, rightfully in the end, drool !!!
Yes, The Heavenly trail similar to school
Housing many, old and new
Awarding each according to person's move
Regarding The Heavenly trail likened to a school
Where all, required to obey rules

When another gladly pays fees due
The Heavenly Institution
Only judiciary without jurisdiction
Hallmarks, of boundless intuition
Heavenly trail school
Allowing free swim in pool
Without threatening precious cool
The amazing Heavenly trail school
Provides all, including books
To enjoy Holy Eternal Foods !!!
The Heavenly walk, perfect school
Bleaches away deadly moods

Adorned with refreshed angelic looks
Can only be The Heavenly school
Pulling us out of the woods
And placed on Gracious Golden Stool
The amazing Heavenly school
With us, has genuinely stood
Side by side in trials to soothe
Not just anyone leads Heavenly school
But one, Heavenly moved
To us, deceptively woo
Never look like, of Heavenly school
When they spoke, never understood
But the HUMBLE, helped to remain drooled
In the trail called The Heavenly school
Ensuring chances they don't rue
In us, all motivation is fused
Who wouldn't want to attend this school?
For sticking with what you knew
Would not guarantee hope for any few
Favourite meal, anything with rice
With age, should change or pay heavy price
If not, will I always be right?
Appreciating God, by what we have
Knowing in life, change is required !!!
Sticking with old routine, will it not cut !!!
I attended school for many years
Could I remain there, in grey beard ?
Use knowledge for fruitful works

MESSIAH RETURN NIGH, WORLD, IS NOW REAL
LET PREPARATIONS, EMBRACE BESPOKE DEAL
SO, ARRIVAL, ACTION DEMONSTRATE SEALED
ELEVATED, AS CHANGED PRODIGALS REGAIN
CORRECTING EACH MISTAKE ALREADY MADE
NEW CREATION, HEAVENLY MEALS, IN PLACE
YES, NOW CHANGED, FROM ONCE GRUESOME
INTO, ETERNAL, HEAVEN ONENESS, BLOSSOM
IN HIM, DEPICTING, INEXPLICABLY, WINSOME
LET'S GRAB, THIS, WITH BOTH HANDS, WORLD

There comes a time, when, should let go !!!
Let go, of non-profitable old
So, what we love, won't become woes !!!
Should know when to let go
Let go to save own soul
Religious leaders, admittedly, don't know!!!
"No one knows", routine chorus, obviously imperfect
One, who knows, Heavenly accredited
Such, in Heaven, always direct, perfect
Now, not for erratic talk, fame, fortune
Seeking Heavenly comfort, not worldly tycoons
Who knows, worldly, no advantage as moguls
There are times when we should let go
Of what we are unsure being bold
Having not received answers to telling goals
That time is now, to let go
What eventually destroys lifetime shoal
For, Heaven seals individually, every soul !!!

Only in Heavenly school
When evil, ready to all, away scoop
Steps in, humble obedient, safely swoop
Humans, typically, refuse certain changes
Not when it comes to particular stages
We accept, suitable ones at certain phases !!!
For development, we should change !!!
Looking back on hurdles, in our wake
Forward thinking, our only gauge
Many drink unhealthy water !!!
Should they refuse resolution to matter?
Or remain to falter
Red alert, threat by hurricane !!!
Should you move or stay?
Staying, what becomes your fate?
Should let go, the rubbish
For, well-being, be bullish
Not to regret, for being foolish
What we hold onto, never be all end all
Knowingly, we need change, to rightly score
May be into unknown, but definitely not a bore !!!
Should you remain, because all you know is abuse?
Up to you, to refuse
Sad, if opportunity, not put to good use!!!

Was a revelation, advent of radio !!!
How many know, to showcase from patios?
Will not be high, judged on ratio
Why, because, outmoded !!!

Something more entertaining, moulded !!!
Life's fate, soon, to be folded!!!
Should seek, accept change, with time
Else, won't be left, a dime !!!
For time, no longer on our side
Having naturally grown
So, time has also flown
Past seeds, we've previously sown
Businesses fail, lacking foresight
Without right expertise, to strategize
Not just our thoughts, but customers desires!!!
The Heavens who created the earth
Knows what we require from birth
Providing what we needed even unto death !!!
Should we refuse Heaven regarding our hereafter?
Is there anyone who knows better ?
No one has better deal, regarding barter !!!
Many "RICH" wished for something better
At least to live better, farther
But no machine renders that answer !!!
Many wished they could buy eternity !!!
Heaven refutes this richness as prosperity
Has own, unrivalled, quality
The kind, humans cannot create !!!
For, if we did, we would sadly erase !!!
Saying, with our hands, we have greatly made !!!
That quality, humans cannot reach
For His requirements, we would breach
Hence, destitution, we continually preach !!!
One thing, having good intentions

Another, practicing Heavenly reflections
Not under any of our retentions !!!
We are centuries away from home !!!
For world has heart of stone !!!
Without glow, leading to The Throne !!!
We're weary, yet nowhere near home
Night, very dark, cold
Wherefore any glimpse of hope ?
In near fatal accident, yet far from home
Who relieves, of this yoke?
Answer, verily, beyond our scope
World, like rats
Feeding off remains dumped
Thinking, would always survive on scraps

Again, slumbered world, like rats
Enjoying, feeding off other people's plans
One day, goes, and trapped
There come mention of miracles
Surrounded by deadly tentacles
So, anything Heavenly trivial, a spectacle
We do genuinely experience certain encounters
Those I call Heavenly prompters !!!
For, we cannot go far, with human tutors !!!
Wake-up calls come, when masses in evil pre-occupied !!!
Even though occupation won't survive !!!
So, awake world, find a place to hide !!!
Truly, they do come, when we are self-obsessed
Not realizing we're demon possessed
But sadly, thinking we're Heavenly addressed

Wake-up calls come, when we feel self-obsessed
Without realizing, demon possessed, can only retrogress
Then, sorrowful, with fatal regrets
Wake up calls come, when, cautiously, feeling confident
In what we assume, is Heavenly providence
To rationalize significantly we displayed impertinence
Wake-up calls come when paper money takes precedence !!!
Fabric of life revolving around its presence
Losing therefore, Heavenly residence!!!
We don't realize it, when fully involved
Marriages around it, revolve
Selling dignity, for WASTE to resolve !!!
Yet, asleep world, never seem to learn
Losing dignity to, it, earn
More we earn, more we yearn
Loyalty destroyed because of paper money
Yet, truly, never seem to have any !!!
Though, worldly, destroying so many
We never use others' examples
Until we're used as the samples
Yet, to asleep world, never ample
We destroy everything for its pursuit
Even when we realize it doesn't suit
Doing it, for everyone says, it's a perfect suit
Oh, this sick and sinking world
When needy, agrees to a good weld
When okay, changes about how he felt
"The welder did not do a great job"
In fact, blocking his chance to the top
Oh, how he could sadly sob !!!

The welder, Saviour of no use!!!
Found another with plenty of goods
Deserve better than those smelly foods
The world, begging to be accepted
Now claims, has rather been intercepted
Seeking divorce, every offer, rejected
The world, without a leg, on which to stand
Now running with fast strong stamps
Thinking, sky the limit, the destined stance !!!
Would this world have nerve to realise mistakes?
For Heaven to consider the stakes?
Awake world, bad taste will be our steak
Heaven has done lots and more for this world
Yet, it will not accept Heavenly word
So, facing death, right here on earth !!!...

Change, for Salvation

This naïve world calls gold precious !!!
Not realizing, it is oh so precocious
Gold will not be fooled into being so rebellious
This naïve world calls diamonds, pearls
Anyone who has, so, accordingly, purrs
Real pearl, not kept in purse
This ungrateful world adores all mineral ores
Dying for them, in foul-scenting awe
Only to realize, they're not what we wished for
Our sad world pursues all that glitters
The very same, that gives us the jitters
All heading for voluminous litters !!!

The love for death
Which we've chosen instead
Has prepared our beds
Desire for infinite death
So profound, we cannot tell its depth
In its path, we've all delved
Our delight in death
In whose path we always step
Won't wipe the tears we shed
The desire for death, making all harlots
Makes us believe we're hot-shots
Until we realize, we're "Cold-Pulse."
"Cold Pulse", world, wherefore your flaunts?
Borrowed time, wherefore your paraded fronts?
When, to smile, costs money up-front
Now then, wherefore your foolish pride?
When you thought no one man deserves your prize
No longer worthy of any notable price
"Cold Pulse", where is your fame?
The world has denounced you to become lame
Oh what a shame, could you ever be tamed?

When "Cold Pulse" fails, that is "Cold Pulse."
"I, for one, never been false"
Till death grabs, with its deadly paws !!!
Heaven has upped the stakes!!!
Nothing a gamble, like lottery staked !!!
Nor as easy-peasy, enjoying steaks
"Cold Pulse tragedy, that is "Cold Pulse."
Will always gather loins before rain pours

The rain came, and all were left on lawns
Detailed worldly mishaps, "Cold-Pulse's" doing
Saying you're married yet one else, you're seeing
And again, who do you think you're deceiving?
No difference between us and "Cold-Pulse's." !!!
All our pulses beat according to evil's forces
Sadly, we don't realize to hold horses
What can I say, about this selfish world?
Who refuses Heaven's Holy word?
But desires Heaven's Heavenly reward?
What can I say about this greedy world !!!
When with evil, have we strongly merged
But desire comforts, as Heavenly weld
What's to say, not foretelling occurrences in the day
For, only thing working, games we play !!!.
Non trustworthy, mainstay
No one prepared to forgo
But all desire The Heavenly goal !!!
Two masters won't shape one soul!!!
No one wants to let go
But, say desire The Heavenly road
Wait till served to giant toads
Everyone thinks he is right
Without realizing the plight
Until sadly, there can't be a flight
Everyone assumes charged under Heavenly vaults!!!
All acclaim the flight of a catapult
When really talking about pole vault
No one wants to forgo evil nature !!!
Wanting Heaven, thinking, have enough stature

Very sad, deceitful posture
A man can make a difference !!!
In our pathetic lives, there is the evidence
Who then under-estimates Heavenly presence
One man makes a huge difference !!!
Most cases, not a pretence
Transcending all, seeking indulgence

The Heavenly messenger, all, everything transcends
From The Heavens, with message, descends
After delivering, accordingly, ascends
How long He stays, He transcends
Incorporating all, who don't pretend
Embracing all, adoring His presence
All hearts start, equally, to transcend
Message piercing hearts to rightly represent
Following the message, near or far from His residence
All boundaries, Heavenly message, transcends
Before Him, nothing takes precedence
Because He renders absolute providence!!!
Heavenly message, ultimately, everything transcends
On the cusp of hell, there is proficience !!!
His timely message, one can call, coincidence
None is above death !!!
The Heavenly trail we all need to search
For our just, just don't help
Heaven appreciates asleep world's weaknesses
Especially, regarding businesses
Global warming, Heavenly message supersedes all
preparedness

We're supposed to be in Heavenly gold-fish bowl
But haven't managed it, like The Heavenly folks
When are we due back into that Heavenly role?
The Heavenly message remains in the middle
To resolve Heavenly riddle
To those who receive it, a real sizzle!!!
The message in this house
Carries plenty of laughs
The same that helps reach enviable heights !!!
Heavenly message, comes with fun
The only one to lead under the sun
With legs, humanity can't run!!
The Heavenly come with a smirk
Enjoying life in it, standing firm
We all, obviously, need more work
This Heavenly message, a brilliant melody
Enjoying it, definite synchronized methodology
The best green to experience in ecology
We really require steely guts
Once decided, there are no buts
Not to gain, will only be nuts
The Heavenly message, the real beginning of life
Who is ready, can only see The Heavenly light
Embracing this chance, with every bit of might !!!
Man's life's continuation here-on
Working hard, from dusk to dawn
Onto the land, of the healthiest corn

Inherited religions haven't lived up to standards !!!
Asleep world, assumed it on snap chats

Awake, place to be, number one on Heavenly charts
Religion dwells on previous saintly laurels
Making us live like live empty barrels
Horses are here, let's get onto readied saddles !!!
Because of sin, we're all under skids
From elderly, to kids
We should throw all evil-doing in skips
The Heavenly get us motoring
Really very motivating
All disparities, we should be removing
The world seeks what it cannot grab
Yet, what is at hand it can't have
Because, it is eating its cake to have one
The opportunity, money cannot buy
We shouldn't let pass by
Sad, with non-interest, He says good bye
History for us today, not on our side
Known to receiving The Heavens with spite
To our favour, should we shift this tide
Accepting the woe, in which manner?
Is it to be with a murmur?
For message ignored means gravely murder

Malnourished Humans Seek Death

No better food than Heavenly manna !!!
From it, should no one, do a runner
To enjoy green everlasting summer
Undeniably, no better food than Heavenly manna
May, initially taste bitter, no matter

Would be yearning for more, times later
Yes, to our deadly ways, have we been tied
Let's give ourselves chance to say, yes we tried
For, finally, we'll enjoy the ride
A, once in a lifetime exposure
Question marks about our current disclosure
Heavenly message, renders perfect enclosure
This message, definitely doesn't woo
Doesn't matter if one decides to boo
For when needed, you'll run for the loo !!!
All stuck in a pit
With all, just not fit !!!
The Heavenly message, provides the kits
The indiscriminate message which to all, fits
Only revealed to who HUMBLY sits
So, to The Heavens, hearts would be eternally lit !!!

No question, into The Heavens we do not fit
The evil message, our hearts have already hit
Mama wished, wished she didn't have a tit!!!
In our heart of hearts, we continually lie
Serious lack, that is sure on our file
Heavenly, everyone enjoys each one's warm tie
We have to grow quickly with this manure
I know, not easy, obliged world unsure
But with open hearts, we'll soon be mature
Our ways put us in Heavenly debt
Need to reverse, re-invest
Becoming in Heavenly eyes, excellent
We've a lot to be thankful for

Not those we put at the fore
But those that to life, is core
Focusing on big money business, not best
Not knowing how we awake from beds
Evidence, that on wrong horses, we place bets
Yes, seeming to realize a Deity
Yet, not portraying relative responsibility
Abusing foundations of humanity
Let's appreciate breathing, seeing, hearing, etc., not gold !!!
How blood, air, water, food, waste etc, in us flow
Hair, limbs, tissues, teeth, bones etc., ceaselessly grow
When we digest these, we lift Him in awe !!!
Hurting another, would never dawn
These important utilities, we all pawn
How body is protected from hair to sole
Maintaining walking about with precious soul
Doing this together, none left alone!!!
Even how we are formed, metal, bones and tissue
Something to think about, important issue
Our lovely fellow humans we shouldn't misuse
Wrong choices, about using resources
Knowing all has been for the negative forces
Hastily, should revert to the Heavenly causes
From time, He detests our so-called gifts
Prompting us, we still don't blink
We should re-awake and re-think !!!
Our useless importance, we should denounce
The Heavenly adorable, to spiritually announce
Not by mouth, but actions, pronounce
Starting, being humble to inner beings

Holiness foundation, not earthly feelings
Human of Heaven oozing humility, not sweetening
Heavenly angels carry Holiness with them
We ignorantly uphold their memories as emblems
When gone, oh, only if we knew, then!!!

But we abuse and torture The Holy
Because of our ignorant folly
Not realizing that we are rather phoney
Self-respect, very important!!!
Grabbing opportunity to Heaven, becoming a constant
No religion better than obtaining Heavenly insurance
Our activities should be portraying divine Islam
To move away from spiritual slums
So that evil, we'll eternally slam!!!
Should portray improved Christianity
The like, that acquires Heavenly identity
For an everlasting nobility
No shortfalls either regarding Judaism
To boldly demonstrate divinity without satanism
All others shunning individualism
Everyone, today, uses smart-phones
Let's all get Heavenly ones to call home
So, on response, we would gather more hope
We should live as humble Heavenly ministers
Showing dedication and obedience as administrators
To communities as benefactors
The world today is going inclusion
With a perfect communal reason
Having all failed in our missionary mission

Innovation, inclusion, individualism etc., gathering pace
So, the farther away The heavenly Grace
Because of the societal general mental state
Innovation, inclusion, individualism etc, a subdued divide
Which when exploding, will cause untold fright
I wonder how many of us , this, will suffice?
No one in the eyes of Heaven acts right
We're all always provoking a fight
Why religion is Heavenly, not out of sight
Religion, source of us, divisive
Yet, all stuck in it, so decisive !!!
While Heavenly greats, incisive
Woe unto us, of The Heavenly anger
No one authority, power, status, does a runner
Should all do a U-Turn, before thrown asunder
Sweeping Heavenly issues under the carpet
Because our sins we love to protect
Causing, permanent Heavenly defect
Wake up world, have duties to perform
To undergo uplifting Heavenly reforms
Then, spiritually claim, in top form
We can do it if we want
No longer saying we can't
Let's try harder, before we're sunk

Question is, where do we get it from?
How do you receive this Heavenly prompt?
It cannot just be a front
JESUS led the apostles, others, it worked
They helped community, some turned

Because, Heavenly, their bellies churned
Some time elapsed, Mohammed surfaced
Because what existed, out of place
For, Heavenly qualities, was a waste
There was change before JESUS, Mohammed
Always change from here, there
Will continue from breath to death
Change is inevitable for daily development
No one stays in year one to receive upliftment
Should climb to next level, for growth supplement
In my Heavenly Father will I always wallow
For He knows I'm not empty, hollow
To be one, I wished, to follow
Yes, this is what's known all these years
But, now, comes with fears
Won't I want to change to avoid tears?
Chicken and egg issue, Heaven, does not exist
Creating all animals to live
Currently, all Heavenly, yet not inclusive !!!
If we do this always
With ONENESS touching Heavenly lanes
What role then, does religion play?

The Rail Replacement Driver

When rail replacement occurs
Implies, the norm, actually suffers!!!
Time for essential engaging repairs
Once rail replacement occurs
Resolving situation falling into tatters

As instructs management upstairs
In case a rail replacement happens
Many spirits become dampened
Creating confusion, others, looking burdened
Because some distinct change has occurred
The normal routine, seemingly referred
Plans for new, old system perturbed
When a rail replacement occurs
Driver follows instruction from experts
Services abound for who accordingly dares
With own tools, comes prepared
Driver takes no fares
A to B, all that matters
On day rail replacement occurs
Driver doesn't use route normally preferred
Different transport, carrying all there
With cost of replacement incurred
New driver shows He cares
On time, awaiting passengers
Placed at required station
Planned, made for all to destinations
Routines abandoned for another occasion
Arriving at stops, different from previous one
Scheduled accordingly, with own plan
Up to us, to do what He says and wants
Doesn't have plenty of time to delay
Whatever his instructions, that, he relays
For a short time, starting from today

Heavenly replacement driver, not even identified
Yet, in Him, could all be satisfied
Abandoning old routines, Heavenly, numbers becoming multiplied
The Heavenly replacement driver needs none funny
Ready to take as many
Assuming role of humble nanny
Heavenly replacement driver, ready to embrace
Who identifies Him, to cut the chase
Fulfilling outstretched arm of empty space
Professional driver will take all
Yet, on His bus, you are not a doll
He ensures, you are alert, can't be dull
Sticking to planned, specific times
Delays cost more than a dime
None tolerate unnecessary delays at times, prime
With driver ordered from top
Own tale, taking Him for a mob
Doesn't care if He is less than a dot !!!
When the replacement bus stationed
Not many knew, would be positioned
People ward off, with hasty decisions
He surely does not look like the norm
His starting and finishing doesn't last long
Comes, does job, short period, gone
When the Heavenly angel appears in human form
Implies, something, seriously wrong
Needing addressing, before getting out of sorts!!!

Time, Is Now

Only few ably do this
Not case of hits and misses
But from the tried, tested, right thesis
In all these, there is one word we're all missing
One word missing from daily listings
We've failed our listings for not listening
Demonstrating how we're growing, sinking !!!
Sinking because growing in sin, evident feeling!!!
Feeling of missing out, really happening
We have our religions, families, businesses etcetera
What more, as extra
Reaching sky, showing diaspora?
What are we seeking, we're not finding?
We quote Allah, God, Yahweh, Bapu, etc, commanding
So, the basis of other in whom we're confiding?
What then is causing so much mess in our lives?
Are we reaping what we've sown in lies?
Or reality, checked out on us, hypocritical ones !!!
Crucially lacking, yet, claim we have it all
Individually, collectively, not standing tall
So-called good deeds leading to evident fall
Because, from top to bottom, something isn't right
Sending out chilling, obvious fright
Fearing for all of us, approaching strike
For, we've lost main ingredient !!!
Relationships, fundamentally, non-existent !!!
Even, same religion, not consistent !!!

We've forgone the main ingredient !!!
Fundamental family ties insufficient
Still, same parents, religion, very deficient !!!
We've lost the cornerstone !!!
The focal ingredient, building a home !!!
Replacing, with litter, we call gold
We've lost the Heavenly Father !!!
Deceiving ourselves with beliefs, shifting us wilder
For, in Him, would all be calmer
Yes, we've lost the Heavenly Father
Focusing on famous money, creating disaster
Same parent siblings, religion, killing one another
Now, benchmark for success, Father !!!
Man of wisdom fumbles because of it, Pastor
Everyone's head is turned for your litter, Leader
Even the physical stature, prefer another's body
Feeling, what we have, shoddy
Rather, the dreaded, correlating orchestral melody
Let's forget what we think we have, for now
And into our deepest hearts, should we plough
And ask if The Creator of all, is proud?

Let us sit back into our souls, intently
Searching ourselves really thoroughly
And ask if The Greatest Almighty agrees happily
The world seeks what it cannot find
Yet, what it finds, it doesn't want
Due to sheer ignorance
Therefore chasing magical wand

Using wicked approach for Heavenly fact
How is it going to change for everlasting pact?
The world seeks what it is beyond reach
For the saintly traits it has breached
Yet, not ready to relinquish visits to beach
Frustratingly, pursues what it won't feel
Because evil feel, won't peel
Yet assumes Heaven automatically heals
Slumbered world seeks what is beyond real
Because of obscene rate at death's wheel
Where abounds disaster as an open field
Craving for what is not real
From generation to generation, won't deal
In deals of Eternal Heavenly feel
World, seeking good, destroys good
Insane or ignorantly, cool
Tearing apart foundations of Living Food
Desperate for Heaven, yet, destroying Heaven
Why doesn't see and know, can't imagine
For, times on end, confirms the brethren
What world seeks, can only be gloom
For our good, only assumed
Founded upon deceitful groom !!!
Some counterfeits, difficult to detect
Especially, when all really appears perfect
Heavenly opposition, seen as traitor, defect !!!
The pot, already boiling
Temperatures, extremely soaring
Intended heart desires, already pouring
Pot's already boiling

Off-springs already coiling
The white robes, so badly soiling
Worldly pot, already boiling
Umbilical cord remnant, crawling
Mum feeding babies, who come calling
When cup of tea, already drank
Not easy to accept, a prank
Knowing proceeds only draw blank
Cup of tea, already drunk
Cannot separate tea, water, from belly bank
Going to work, once sunk

When content already sipped
Feeling taste of cream, whipped
Until after work, then tipped
Accepting everlasting fate
Unpopularly, truly at stake
For blindness, us, has upstaged
Bowing to our eternal fate
From our enemies as darling dates
Our dilemma, no mere fakes
For what comes out of us
What we've concluded as ours
Strategically planted as guiding oars
Yes, what comes out of us
What we've passionately addressed
As path rendering eternal rest
Everyone knows the word!!!
Reading and listening to what is said
From pastor to church, no one a third

Everyone knows about the word!!!
Discussed at "holy places", to all it's served
In their view, they're blessed

Town Crier at Work

If JESUS has descended today?
Who wouldn't spit into His Face?
Like previous, assuming Him gay !!!
Emphasising, JESUS back again today
What have we got to say?
To try convincing Him we're okay
Should He be on earth today?
What part are we going to play?
Convincing positive display?
If eventually shown up on earth today?
Sure we won't say, nay?
Can't be our price to pay !!!
Having, The Saviour back to save
World, able to understand The Way?
The apostles endured, to be, for us, hooray!!!
Forget assumptions, JESUS is back again
Would we be able to take?
The parables He continually says?
The Messiah is here with His message!!!
Would we be able to trade?
All church activities absorbed to date?

Yes, debatably, JESUS, back again today
How, to ascertain?

Him, helper for Heaven to attain?
The Light on our path is here to regain!!!
How are we going to maintain
Love attached to His Holy name?
Town crier, asserts, Redeemer here today
What is the basis for our delay
As One to show The way?
No imaginations here, JESUS arrives today
Being the one leading others to pray
How, becoming one of His dates?
Suddenly, He appears again today
Heavenly nous required, for ways, to be paved
To walk His talk, truly saved
Suddenly, Promised lamb shows up today
Vacating posts to be changed?
Heavenly angels, us, to embrace?
Unknowing road rage with one today
Important meeting, so in haste
Finding attacked wrongfully decides fate !!!
One needing help with flat tyres, JESUS today
Blowing horn, ushering Him out of your lane
Later, you, in accident, recognising, Him to save !!!
Raining insults on The Word, cruelly, today
Not fitting in lavish ways
Beaten up, bleeding, your surgery bill He pays !!!
Snatching Heavenly one's mobile, today
Calling you back, saying
Cease this worthless business to be saved!!!
Overdue time, meeting JESUS, these days
Directing lives without wicked ways

For, humans and animals, feeding on same hay
Christian, meets JESUS, face-to-face
Church, to forsake?
So, timely, parables, He interprets?
Devout Muslim bumps into JESUS, today
The Koran, willingly put away?
Living Heavenly, night and day?
Self-righteous Jew meeting JESUS today
Yes, all Ten Commandments from birth obeyed
Forgo treasure, for Heaven, to acknowledge your name?
Hindu, bumping into JESU, ready to abandon all sayings?
Conforming to new, controversial adages
To acquire sustainable Heavenly wages?
Oh, we of nothing Heavenly, faith
Full of messy meaningless bathe
When do we expect to all drain and shave

Imagine preacher, meeting JESUS today
Will you leave congregation to say
Found One, who is The Way??
Life's, positively a trail
Yet, depending upon chosen train
Humility helps to prevail
Life, has to be a trail
Yet, can receive Heavenly mails
Being in Heavenly domains
Life, meant to be eternity
Having The Way to infinity
Guarantees earthly Heavenly Divinity
Hence, never designed to be easy

Bound to feel wheezy
Don't be in frenzy
Awake, world, talking life eternity!!!
Can never be easy treaty
Death traps, all over vicinity
Wake up to eternal strategy
Will never be easy duty
Worthless ones, taking eternity
Scraping off years of dirt a trail
Ha, so chin up on this rail
If truly desiring Heavenly ale
So consumed, are we, even in ambiguity
Not ready for a step back, from rotten integrity
Should be time for Heavenly Eternity !!!
Top nations do nothing for free !!!
Avoid anyone teaching Heavenly glee
Lavishing in worldly riches, anti The Holy Tree
JESUS never sought riches of this world
Peter, apostles, empty, boasted in the Word !!!
Silver, gold, they had not, yet, verily, they fared
All, therefore, loving bearing their names
Without realizing, criminally insane !!!
Stealing Heavenly identity, all should refrain !!!
Names came with anointed responsibilities !!!
Oozing Heavenly feel, in their identities
Tasks Heavenly designed, with armoured capabilities !!!
Even with Bible, addressing, One Pastor
Wonder how people, think, they give pasture !!!
The Heavens angrily roaring, it is past time !!!
Yes, overdue for hanky-panky stuff !!!

If really in-depth, this, no bluff !!!
No other way declaring, all of unheavenly staff !!!
The prophets, without "Holy Books" for a reason !!!
To engrain words in hearts, like them, not preaching !!!
For He Himself knocking on hearts for teaching !!!

The kind, Only He, JESUS, does !!!
The type, Only He knows, and wants
The One Touch Healing, Eternally stands
Not the money-spinning brand
Destroying homes because we're blind
Lavishly eating from trees we didn't plant
Millions of miles away from truth !!!
Enjoying the worldly lying fruit
Thinking, no alternative, join the loot !!!
Parents can't smack kids
But adults punch others off their skids !!!
For lives can be exchanged for quid
Can we not, seriously, have better alternatives
Like big boys in football competitions
Long-term better ways of enjoying relatives
Let's learn from toddlers !!!
We, supposed leaders !!!
Rather the spoilers !!!
Let's learn from our children
Self-glorified brethren
Learn from Sanhedrin
Needing to mature from our children
Instead of wasting on pilgrims
Assuming, all well, with Heaven

Seriously, let's learn from young youngsters
Developing into gangsters
As happy-go-merry characters
Each plays with each other
Without slightest bother
Seeing each as sister and brother
They're so innocent in their ways
We physically evidently need The Grace !!!
To know that Heaven is not a place !!!
No, Heaven, not a place, nay
Banging our heads without His displays
Know now, religion, has all, displaced !!!
Like previous, Heaven completely misunderstood !!!
Mentality, activities, don't bear Heavenly fruits !!!
Any critic, appears to this world, of no use
All trying to acquire, what we're ignorant of
For our understanding and Heaven, way off
Blighted and crippled by own worldly font
Desperate to save what is left
Yet, all strategic moves, backward steps
Even knowledgeable, admitting seeing the worst
Salvation message, never received in arrogance !!!
Yet, all full of it, calling it repentance !!!
Repentance from evil to innovative evil, no Heavenly chance

The chance to receive available since creation !!!
Creator always differently made available salvation
Yet, world sees redemption pathway as condemnation
Any condemnation, our perceptions
Perception for not containing true confessions

Confession that grabs, growing Heavenly intentions !!!
Who knows, when all, seeking, pleasures?
Busily, building, naming, useless treasures !!!
With categorically, "No one serves two masters", measures
"No one serves two masters", dangerous situation
Diabolical situation for all including congregations
Ignorant congregation, oiling, dire implications
Implication of The Heaven and Eternity really is
JESUS isn't stupid to come, work, stay empty like this?
The Way, that His team didn't find, a nemesis
Having the life and vision of Heaven here !!!
Greatest Teacher laid it bare and explicitly clear !!!
So clearly, when followed, seen as weird
So, WUOW, pursuing what we cannot find
Not equipped with appropriate fund
Thinking, we'll always have fun !!!
Owner of the world, raging, furious
For our ways, dubious
Wake-up call, making a few curious
Yes, curious of what possibly could be
Worse than one attacked by billions of bees !!!
Failing, to even pay earthly fees
With what then, do we seek The Heavens?
When continually refusing learning lessons?
The only Saviour, we're always messing
Message, because of mess of this age !!!
This "age" thinks, above the "be careful" stage
Why, thinking The Messenger will be upstaged!!!
The messenger, what's the detailed message?
Our lives to Heaven, like that of the ice age

For the message, to Heaven not even the first page !!!
Why all researchers, religious chiefs still searching ?
Searching for answers yet not reaching.
Reaching to apps, operating, dangerous trending
No. rumour-mongering folks!!!
The dead burying dead in droves
Music, preaching, movies, selling, raising hopes

Raising hopes, assumption, on right track
A deceit, nothing The Heavens accepted as brand
Made, accepted on evil ground
Riches increase, the world craves
Who, even has authority to say, good morning, a craze !!!
What good has one borne, living in evil, a daze !!!
We enjoy calling, good, blessing, shots
Yet, all have lived, worked, for evil plots
Who is savvy enough to wake to these exploits
We enjoy calling the good and blessing shots
Operating on huge Heavenly void
We only hiss out deadly blood clots
To have good blessing acceptable shots
Let's firstly cleanse inner blots
In the love of the Heavenly Lord
Yet, to all the rubbish, apostles, not enticed
Sticking to The Heavenly, solely on the minds
Enjoying worthy Heavenly, in which He beguiles

THE TIME IS NOW, TOWN-CRIER HAS REVEALED
SHOW, HE IS, TO BE IDENTIFIED AND BELIEVED
SALVATION IS READY TO EAT HEAVENLY MADE

RAIL REPLACEMENT DRIVER, HEAVENLY AGAIN
MALNOURISHED FEEDING, HEAVENLY TO SEAL
WHO WANTS, CHANGE DIET, ENJOY, THIS PLACE
VOID IS NO LONGER UNDER SOME DISCUSSIONS
EXCEPT, IN HEAVENLY ONENESS, ALL BLOSSOM
IN HIM, IS BECOMING INEXPLICABLY, WINSOME,
YES, TIME TO WAKE UP, CHANGE TONE, WORLD

When JESUS washed the apostles' feet,
Indication, they were totally clean,
A sure sign, of absolute humility
This apostles' feet washing feat
He was relaying to Heaven, that they were neat
Heaven, could call them clean
When JESUS washed the apostles feet
He prepared them with the baton to lead
A vital ingredient, they would always need
Symbolic act of washing apostles' feet
Tells Heaven, they're on their knees
Those allowed, to enjoy Heavenly treat
Yes, JESUS washed the apostles feet
Those who sacrificed all their needs
As toast of Heavenly deeds
Leader's humble deed cleansed, including feet
When He knew their inside were first clean
Proving, they're ready indeed
Also, demonstrating His absolute humility
The top quality, for total divinity
In the approved Heavenly community
We build houses from the roof

Thinking it will stand on the ground with the wood
Because our brains are not Heavenly tuned

Who lives in a house without paying rent for a year,
Five, ten, twenty, fifty, seventy, years, dear
Heaven has allowed us, over 2000 years
Living for so many years without paying rent
Picking and choosing anywhere, to pitch tents
Leaving everywhere dirty, with foul scent
Refusing to pay, He wants us all out
Into the world, has He sent scouts
Who have reported to Him of how we scrounge
Reporting back, what they found
None worth a single pound
In the soul, body, mind, not sound
Bodies, never good, using His facilities.
Refusing making use of opportunities
Yet, daily, yearly, continuing absurd destitution
Building houses on wrong foundation
So, no matter Heavenly visitation
Never equipped for included nomination
There was every physical evidence
Not requiring impudence, impertinence, insolence
We've forfeited Heavenly innocence

CHAPTER TEN

Worldly Concerns

WORLDLY CONCERNS WILL SURELY PERSIST
UNTIL EVIL NATURE WE ETERNALLY RESIST
FROM BAD DELICACIES WE UTTERLY DESIST
A MUST FROM VERY LEAST TO FILTHY ELITE
NO JOKES HERE SKINT, YET, ASSUMED RICH
FROM ATHEIST TO ANGEL, HE TRANSCENDS
PREVIOUS ONES HEARD AND GRABBED HIM
RABBI, PASTOR, IMAM, ELIMINATE BAD VIMS
TO EMBRACING TRUTHFUL HEAVENLY WITS
COVID, OTHERS, STARTERS, AWAKE, WORLD

Whatever the trouble, worry, wobble
With an in-depth remorse doubled
Heaven makes sorting, no trouble
Yet, the world constantly in rage
Raging to mount the stage
A rate to pay homage
But, homage, who to?
To whom is it really due?

The move with doom?
Yes, he operates as light
Having something which is slight
We, sadly think is absolute might
Yes, he has a part to play
With those in his domain
But The Lord's, he cannot slay

The world likes to show off
Heaven boasts, in rebuff
Displaying beyond doubt, His, are tough
Prophets suffered for years on end
Prepared to suffer for longer extent
The prize, we just cannot comprehend
Who has strength to portray endurance?
Who, the mantle to display sustenance?
Who, the will to uphold resistance?
Who displays evil's defiance?
Who oozes Heavenly countenance?
Who relays Heavenly resonance?
All, in boastful hurry
To display from the quarry
Gem duly thinking they carry
None patiently waiting
Hurrying to display emptiness at pace,
Greatest value of their taste
All, dying from "I'm better than you", syndrome
Pushing into oblivion, preferred gnomes
Greedily grabbing all "riches" in droves
Losing cool heads because of foolish pride

Thinking, must grab, as feels right
No matter effect on brother's plight
"I am better than you", all aspects of life, insane
Humility cleanses this nonsense in the main
Coaching, building all, to becoming Heavenly names
All say they are vanity, earthly riches
Yet, the same, we flaunt, as blessings
How confused we are in "riches" benediction
"Better than you" sickness, seriously killing all
Ingrained negative competition, what for?
Peanuts, compared with Heavenly installed
While Heavenly quality do not verbally talk
The rest seek to be called
Among, so-called, tall
Yet, without an evening's ball
Wherein lies our joy?
When all is about failing ploys
But, won't withdraw, want to employ
What is destined to us, destroy
When will we realize, not just a decoy

Assailants, our guardians are refreshed
Like flowers in the morning, they are dressed
Glowing like midday sun, they've impressed
Yes, they have been promoted
You are definitely demoted
Failed agenda, you're deflated
The accredited have progressed
You, have painstakingly retrogressed
Now, so madly distressed

Where is your victory?
All you've been, is wizardry
Can only be called painful history
The wicked have no stance
Like chaff, will be gone at a glance
A canoe facing tsunami, no chance
The time is now or never
The Heavenly trail, to discover
Arise, all nations, and deliver
The Heavens has provided a guide
Uploading a worthy guard
Who wants part of this vanguard?
Who looks in a mirror?
Heaven appreciating what he acquired as worker?
Awake world, everyone needs a director
Everyone claims to have a mentor
Yet, all say and know they have no comforter
What is the mission, vision of the conductor?
Again, who is the foolish woman?
Is this the title I want to man?
Far from it, I'll surely run
Who truly is the foolish woman?
Is she already placed in remand?
Or cornered with a death warrant!!!
No one wants to be the foolish woman
Yet, all we do, the evil errand
From topmost evil command
Who doesn't want to be the foolish woman?
Let him, the evil ways, overcome
Meeting The Lord at the rise of the sun

Yet, the entire world, the foolish woman
Savagely wounding everything and everyone
Who wants to avoid this fatal harm?
If not foolish women, what are renowned skills?
Is it the one that kills?
Or, one that rips others off their skins?
Naming our very best skills?
One that educates to the hilt?
Or, one that drowns us, from up close to the hill?

Yes, in terms of our notable skills
The one that renders successful stints?
Or, one that sends one to the mills?
What have we managed to acquire ?
The skills to a high life?
Or ones that melt like ice?
We keep behaving we have valuably revived
An intuition into the Heavenly line?
Or, knowledge that vanishes with time
So, is there something truly acquired?
The thinking that all is well with lies?
Or suffering from pandemic of bodily lice?
When bad is no longer insane
Abominations, promotionally, embraced
Who, really, foretells the next stage?
Cannot imagine, then, trending thrills?
What, world, are our spills
Are they the worldly trips?
How often are thrilling spins?

Are they the Heavenly pills?
Or the hard earned worldly gigs?
What do preachers have to say?
What useful points can you lay?
Are they all not leading to a slay?
Religious leaders have led all to sway
For everyone assumes reasons to stay
Who has lead, to help in Heavenly play?
Who has the Heavenly aromatic spice?
Are these not the works of worldly spies?
Oh, who has the touch to heave up sighs?
Evidently, none seem to have that prize
For, all are clearly full of cries
How they clearly, would be surprised !!!
Who has the rare dream?
To lead the ultimate team?
Want to see some real steam !!!
Their foods contain deadly traces
Consumed without breathing spaces
Who then is at the races?
There are no daisies
No, no sweetly tasting ranges
Who has the formula for the Heavenly pasties?
The Heavenly trail, not a bed of roses
Not calling for any easy doses
No, not period to feel cosy
The worldly thrills, one has to bash
Onto The Heavenly trail in a rush
Who has that instinctive dash?

All have become thrash
For, who, no one has the thrust!!!
All heading for inevitable crush
Who can withstand the worldly sting?
Who is prepared to make a swing?
Who has the ear when The Heavenly ring?
When the orchestrator orchestrates, who sings?
In quicksand, will all, soon sink
Without the energy to swim
Who has ear to heed heavenly calls?
Who displays reactions of Heavenly response?
Nothing moves, even from The Heavenly roar
Who has the ear, surely let him hear
For, not like the worldly, our sins, does He clear
But, afar off some unimaginable, unending rear
Oh how we've all become fools
Hatching joyously in the devil's pool
Embalmed in its deadly wool
Into the worldly pool, all take a swim
Enjoying the daily moves, of being in sync
How can you believe, you will truly sink?
Enjoying the ability to properly swim
Thinking, having skills of the fish, a dink
Wait till you lose breath, wished you stink
Onto the Heavenly course, is the world resentful
Leaders making all wasteful
Who stands out Heavenly tasteful?
All have become careless
All, unknowingly reckless
No, unsurprisingly thoughtless

Everyone has become pointless
Spiritually unbelievably jobless
To all, spiritual food, completely tasteless
Who has qualified indulgence?
If at all, about some confidence
About The Heavenly providence
No one has the honesty
No one qualifies in accountability
All have failed in reliability
Time to receive The Heavenly price !!!
Who has it all in the stride?
Who qualifies with the right pride?
“HE has become my Salvation !!!”
JESUS does not become, Always His notion
Us, accredited, repent into His motion !!!

How we claim self-righteousness !!!
Oh, so quick to claim holiness
Without realizing the depth of our wickedness
The evil call themselves Reverends
Thinking upon the Lord they depend
Only they themselves they commend
How does anyone call himself a Reverend?
When cannot even repent
Because, Heaven can’t be fooled with pretence
When in sin, does not deserve reverence
For, cannot be a meaningful reference
Hence, does not work by obvious vehemence
“Action speaks louder than words”
The saved, live by His Gracious works

No longer under the unwanted curse
But who demonstrates JESUS?
All unknowingly have gone into recess
World, could badly live with regrets

The Worthy Mentor

Denomination against denomination
Religion against religion
Purification against sanctification
So-called chosen, against the neglected
The highly favoured against the rejected
The, "I am better than you", holy blessed
Who is the one, let his works talk
Let his actions be from Heavenly walk
So, with an inventory, a part of the stock
Who is the righteous person?
Does not receive worldly lessons !!!
No, will no longer enjoy unholy processions
A suicidal pill to take
This assumption of Heavenly stakes
Oh, how people will learn to be awake
All are Heavenly, dead-alive
Without Heavenly meaningful life
So, onto Heavenly thought, should we all strive
We innovate into the world
Stressing ourselves unto hell
Defining, with the rotten dead
Everyone born has a nation
Yet, revelling in the Heavenly notion

No, none acknowledged in that motion
Seriously, no one is in tune !!!
Even, in the thought of being in the mood
No one is immune !!!

No tribe, or nation, known to The Heavens !!!
No worldly self-acclaims, have offloaded burdens
For, no one recognises the bread unleavened
Religions don't hold water
No one knows any better
For operations oppose The Humble Master
All religions do not live proper
None in it, Heavenly prosper
This, a very deafening matter
Religion does seriously, not hold water
Old boys' deeds idolised or scatter
Instead of seeking Heavenly plaster
Religious deeds belie Holy ponder
Too many dents, evident in container
No matter the trips, does not serve the builder
Sadly, religion does not hold needed water
For the comfort-seeking deserter
Into books of Heavenly planner
No, sadly doesn't deserve holding water
For the desperately wishing drinker
Desperately coughing and having hiccups
The closest to Heaven has no water
Why, our seasoned wise, will always falter
Yet, Water, we can always get from the Potter
So, should consider reversing trends !!!

Sacrificing everything, to make amends
For, so nigh is the very end
Fasting, prayers, worships, sacrifices, vain
From all these, all should refrain
Keenly pursuing the acceptable new frame
Knowing, "Holy Books", not a bonus
Rather distracts Heavenly focus
On us, then, is eternal onus
Religion, Heavenly prophets never formed one
Never with lying tongue, did He come
But, for ALL to regain Heavenly clan
"Who-so-ever believes in me"
The worthy SEAL of The Almighty, HE
In whom everyone loves to be
"Whosoever believes in me"
From the evil one, will He let him flee
With the smile of Heavenly glee!!!
This is HIM, His words are Him
Everyone for The Heavens, let's trim
From bulging with savage vim
He said "Whosoever believes in me"
The Way, The Truth, The Life indeed
Evil ways make us Heavenly lean

"Whosoever believes in me"
He is categorically, not at all mean
Will know, after stopping evil meals
Inside each of us, The "Heavenly religion"
The Love of The Lord as by the angels
Which should be portrayed with the ancients

Instead, wasting resources on unholy bagels
And showing off unworthy bangles
To the delight of the ignorant bandwagon
"Heavenly religion" journey, only Heaven teaches
Not like in class, to then write thesis
The time is now, to forget meaningless preaching
For every educated, year one was new
But who carries those books to that prove?
"Heavenly religion" to sparkle, only Heavenly approved
Year one acquired Knowledge
Sets up ready for big stage
"Heavenly religion", to develop free, priceless privilege
For in our hearts, should be stored, contents
Wiping away devilish pretence
Growing, therefore, into Heavenly prominence
All meaningful lessons thence, then learnt?
Uprooting hatred unto death!!!
Aren't we supposed to know better, instead?
The brethren, prophets, who teaches them?
Don't they feed directly from The Heavens?
They're examples, not to be worshipped as legends
The world has peaked at finishing line
For with The Heavens, it isn't aligned
Who is ready to shine with this lifeline?
What has become of humans?
We've become lower than animals
Badly lost Heavenly formats
Grew up knowing, animals were, it
But, bit by bit, now, becoming hits
We can't bear fruit with our bits

The Heavens has upped the stakes
The wind, blowing all in its wake
Except who diligently adhered in wait
The Heavens has upped the stakes
Who hasn't bought the worldly bait?
The Heavens knows each at His Gate
All awake to assumed good morning
But, alas, greeted by great mourning
Can only be a serious warning
All awake to meaningless good morning
Worried, among others, global warming
Heated brains, has everyone warring

Without further precious time to waste
On foreheads, The Heavens paste
The hearts that grabbed the word at pace
Being therefore, pathetic lowly troops
Without any thinking pull
Our end, we'll be seeing soon
Sinfully, world, now, rendered spiritually dirty
Living by riverside, yet, unpardonably, thirsty
Lives, muddled and sadly murky
Bloodied hands, don't clean bloodied bodies!!!
Oozing blood every day, talking "porkies"
Abstaining from truth, compounds relentless worries
Only clean hearts, rightly, invade dirt
In the heart, His home, when He gets there
Planting in us, forever, The Humble Word
Sad, managing 100% religious attendance

Yet, don't attain upon guidance
The Heavenly abode, to join the dance
Sad, receiving dedicated religious guidance
Actually, not meriting Heavenly accordance
Change, therefore, is required, for His pursuance !!!
Extremely sad to acquire 100% religious adherence
Yet, not distinct, for Heavenly affordance
So, should adhere, for eternal accordance
The so-called learned, search for clues
Like visiting historical places for roots
Linking to physical proofs
Really? As they do not matter !!!
Digging temporary mulch, instead of The Master?
Hassles, while answers lie on silver-plata
With evil deeds, now, so obvious
Hearing, not, from Heavenly source
What then, achieves Heavenly applause?
Evil, now done on impulse
Forget about foreign imports
Homegrown savagery, we applaud
With naivety making it so obvious
Trending, treading on lost course
Cannot explain, bad occurrences cause
Hence, searching for living among the dead
Will never stand us any good stead
Dead world, lying, on deadly beds
Surely, not about cocaine
This, an even deeper pain
When all signalling, undeniably, insane

Submissive to evil, being heavily drugged
In sin, therefore, are all dragged
Who disconnects from this plugged?

Being hooked onto this killer drug
To hell, each, destined, to drag
For which sake, evil, able to brag
Yes, all heavily addicted to this tonic
World subjected to this antibiotic kick
No strength left, without this cathartic
World has tasted, craves the drug
Which to us, a useful bug
Ending all, deposited, in massive grave bags
Awake, dying for this one cure-all
Whose use is systematically cordial
Leaving us struggling with this portal
We are under this drug
Harmful to the body, it's in the blood
So deadly, no longer a bud
When to us, the heart operates inside
To Heaven, it is on the outside
Our behaviours, that the hearts decide!!!
We can always assume the heart is inside
To The Divine Throne, on our beside
Our attitudes depict where it really resides
As sure as we are that the heart is inside
To The Heavens, we are deprived
Owing to chosen pathetic device
The heart could well be in the body
However, it is outside, displaying fatal trophy

Leaving us inconsolably grumpy
Always holding our heads up in the cloud
Instead of keeping our feet on the ground
For Heaven our focus to mount!!!
Hence, verbally praying to Heaven, never the answer
Not like night out with renounced dancer
No, doesn't cure deadly cancer
Wake up, world, perennial time wasters
Zealous deadly food tasters
Mouths, deeds, portraying Heavenly haters
All arrayed in fine linen
Yet, detesting Heavenly giving
To portray posh living
When The Heavens is my abode
There is none afloat
Who can distract my upload?
Who seeks this assured abode?
Where if you are afloat?
Sharks swim with you like in cosy boat
Always shielded in secure Heavenly abode
To The Heavens and earth would I float
Wondering how many I would coax

Surely not what slumbered world calls abode
Not perceived physical kind to withhold
From the depths of Heaven, has it grown
Open to all, from young to old
Able to take The Heavens' scold
The scold protecting into Heaven's Throne
Who doesn't want this to know?

Heavenly will, freezes all of old
Meeting eternal brothers lo and behold
Tis essential to be updated
Never losing, to be downgraded
Sustaining, to be upgraded
The world went bonkers with plastics
Thinking it was fantastic
Sarcastically, Fanta, not a stick!!!
The world went crazy about plastic
Because it was viably materialistic
Now, not so futuristic
The world was insane with plastic
Now, suicidal mission simplistic
Who has the natural Heavenly mystic?
All assume knowledge, no one raw
Growing, and grown dangerous paws
Devouring and destroying with jaws
All have become healthy bakers !!!
For their organic meals, they have takers
For they, themselves, are real rakers!!!
The clothes of The Heavenly angels they tore
Some, disgracefully, jokingly took and wore
Heaven clearly saw
The Heavenly, we used for a mock
When joke on us, we'll run amok
Evil one's own, won't enjoy his pork
All admit, God is everywhere
Why not, then, worship Him anywhere?
Unless, apart from spiritual leaders', He is nowhere
Admitting God is everywhere

Why have specific places for prayers?
Meaning, He cannot hear, somewhere else?
What if non-accessibility or no longer exist?
Then, The Loving God, would us resist?
Or go to those places, still, we persist?
Our Heavenly God, truly, everywhere
Him in us, we, eternal heir
Counting all marks on bodies, adding hair
Why travelling to specific locations?
Why, thinking those, only sacred places?
When we're the supposed holy destinations

By these practices, inadvertently, limiting God
Same One, we seem so passionate of
Without realizing, we are a long way off
Unless, of course, evident Heavenly visitation
Which develops into Heavenly invitation
The kind that gave apostles' purification
Yes, this sort of angelic descent
To prepare a people, Heavenly decent
We really need, to us, descend
If we could have such, to awaken dying world
Would save at least a few to spread
Some Heavenly good news instead
Would certainly call for a meeting
To be assuredly, then leading
To meeting saints, with Heavenly teachings
But would this myopic world, see?
To accept change, to be invited to tea
The angel would return at speed

We are happy with our "Holy Books"
Gives us the lea-way to fool
Thinking everything is really cool
They were never good enough!!!
Why, Heaven sends angels to make us tough
For all our lives, ignorantly sleeping rough
When, without "Holy Books", there's no life
Supposed wells, in the hearts file
Always refilling, reminding us on our paths
Being therefore, supposed fountains of water
Why, the angels, them, do not carry, ever?
They are, word, sent from The Master
Every word from us, being what The Lord uttered
Not a dot we could have muttered
Demonstrating, our old self, He has slaughtered
Only reserved as reference Books, these "Holy Books"
For the young, needing Holy food
For, without growth, generations on end, of no use
Holding onto them, Sacred, without words in us
But should show The Lord's Love, chewing the cud
Who demonstrates this touch?
Who depicts The Heavenly wave?
Evident in divine peace that saves
Time now, when serving, not even in caves
But, the daily acknowledgement of Heavenly destiny
With class, drawing people into surprised questioning
When, what, how, why is this happening?
All, should step up to the plate
Immersed, not in supposed inclination, but eternal ways
Heavenly attitudinal feel, that wins this case

Collecting previous spiritual physical evidence, a no
Heaven sharply denouncing that know
For, brutalised, never left in peace, it's so
Hence, collecting, adoring legacy, serious misery
Mostly, brothers, sisters, wishing nothing jittery
Nor do they want us badly, dithering
Owed to ourselves, to call Him, JESUS, He would hear
Spiritually stretching forth hands, for He is near
Requiring change, communication, He is always here.
So, wake up world, be that candidate?
Who no longer wishes being obstinate?
Linking with Eternal Ultimate
Prepared to, unto Him, dump all litter
Not willing to anymore dither?
To Him, world, just a sitter !!!
Coming out of scenario, "Polish on dirt"
Out of zone, classified as death
For, among others, we are all deaf
Onto Him, should all our litter dump
We, who are indeed dumb
Dealing with more than just a bump
Getting rid of counterfeit
Dead mode, to quickly forfeit
Avoiding deadly terrible eternal defeat
Getting rid of fatal clutter
According to Heavenly data
Hence, avoiding forthcoming disaster
Humans don't ask telling questions!!!
Quick to make assumed versions

Hastily, drawing conclusions, from wrong assertions
Lifestyles have no time for key questions
Ready to grab popular options
So feeble, with trending sections
Heavenly prophets endured for many years
A few seconds and we're in tears
Confused, in wasteful fears
Who wants to use right spiritual senses?
Looking through Heavenly lenses
Triggering The Heavenly censors!!!
Who prepares with, yes, unto thee, I surrender?
With You, I am ready to go yonder
Living with and in You, forever
Who wants to trigger that providence?
To acquire Heavenly prominence
Enjoying with holy angels', a precedence
For, He is The One who eternally cleanses
Ready for The Heavenly census
The only One who has time for us, dunces

Who wants to be Heavenly divulged?
And then to Heavenly indulge
Who, like me, wants to be involved ?
Could be truly fulfilling karma
Entailing lots of physical drama
To The Heavens a definite, not a comma
World, who possesses such humble intention?
To finally get out of detention
In Ultimate's hands, maintaining a retention !!!
Who flaunts that preconception?

To fall under The Ultimate's detection
Ensuring permanent defection ?
Now, ready for Heavenly implant?
For Heaven to agree, it's a constant
Congratulating, then, as what we warrant !!
Now, ready for Heavenly truth engraft?
The earthly lies, eternally supplant
The real essence of speaking in tongues
For speaking in tongues, not what world performs
Holy Spirit always spoke in tongues, for the records
All about wrongful interpretation, I must inform
Speaking in tongues, really, speaking Heavenly Truth
Mortal world only lie, therefore, truth, always, refute
Misunderstanding, getting the world, sadly bemused
Hence, only The Heavenly agree, from source
Whatever the consequence, at all cost
Should continue upholding eternal course
So, never what naïve world thinks
Lies, ignorance, moving us away from Heavenly link
Yet, thinking, with Heaven, we are in sync
Explaining, apostles, before and after redemption
Hence, ably, living truth, after accredited reconciliation
Pentecostal day, confirms their resurrection

THE WORTHY MENTOR YES ABOUT FOR REAL
NEVER LEAVES HIS, LONELY, WITHOUT DEAL
UP TO WORLD, TO CHANGE, TO SECURE SEAL
SPEAKING IN TONGUES IS HEAVENLY TRUTH
RELIGIONS, LEAD BY EXAMPLE, GET IN TUNE
WITH, HEAVENLY, UNDERSTANDING PROOFS

FOR, HEAVEN ONENESS MAKES US, BLOSSOM
SEEK HIM, BECOME INEXPLICABLY WINSOME
INNOVATE HEAVENLY FOR, WORLD, FADING
HASTEN WORLD, AWAKE, DANGER LOOMING

FROM LITTLE LEAST, TO, RENOWNED, ELITE
THE SKELETON SKINT, TO, THE FILTHY RICH
THE, AGREED ATHEIST, TO TODAY'S, ANGEL
SHOULD, YES, DO, SOMETHING, ABOUT THIS
RIDDING, OF DEVIL ONE'S, DECEPTIVE VIMS
EMBRACE UNIQUE SACRED HEAVENLY WITS
SO, WAKE UP, WAKE UP, AWAKE, OH WORLD

CHAPTER ELEVEN

The Solution, Seek Ye First!!!

World's sin, before Heaven, means, all disabled
Spiritually best at sea, very unstable
How do we get closer to Heaven, ably, stable?
Remembering, all days, He made
Which, right, better, best sabbath day
Immaterial, for, all, different roles, play
Should diligently, Seek, ye, therefore, first…
Heavenly Kingdom birth
If, keen about His worth
Seek ye, therefore, first
Heavenly Kingdom burst
To pass eternal test
Yes, seeking therefore first
Almighty's humility best
Then, sure, to never thirst
With Him first, we are leaders
Dictating pace, as mentors
No one overtaking angelic runners
All going at each one's pace

Task, requirement, determines pace rate
Different start, finish dates of race
Individually required, ye
Alert to respond to names, should we be
As fruits, from responsibilities, portraying deeds
Seek ye first, calls for lifetime dedication
Above full time, long-term supplication
Involving dawn to dusk, vice-versa, implication
JESUS made call, because of His Creed
So, to us, He makes humble plea
Dedicatedly, to Heaven, appeal
Starting, talking in Mary's belly
So, out, He was more than steady
We should quicken, daily ready
Seek ye first, divine plea, beseeching
Roadmap, after evil desires, pleading
Heavenly aperture that yields, to all, motivating

Religion, sadly, sent world into relegation
Disjointed in deceitful devotion
Yielding bad fruit, into revocation
Seek ye first, approach of Heavenly honour
Guiding steady steps, bearing eternal answer
Equipped, armour, fulfilling every prayer
Peacefully to all, in humble unification
Eradicating commotion for harmonisation
Rebuilding chosen, into humble perfection
At different times, ushered into new lives
Encounter, significant for leading onto higher grounds
Bespoke renewed strategy, exciting, with every climb

Accountability, at milestones for each
Systematically accorded despite breach
Co-ordination ensures, none impeached
Waning carnality, waxing spirituality
Breeds steady steely humility
Engrained in daily divine activity
Focusing, on what, one calls, mine
Heavenly shielding, conquers negative minds
Until He, timely unwinds
Hence, mandatory, to do His will
Using every strength, to the hilt
Control, defies human comprehension that wilts
Abundant armoury, cementing inner Lord
For, again, HUMANS do not serve God
Any good acceptable, for one's daily cross
He, the help for anyone who honestly wants
Readily available for anyone who humbly calls
With answers, just a blink from us all
Stepping up required, for His ooze through us
Creating Heavenly environment without tears
Then beginning, portraying, Heavenly mind-set
Growing seeds of joy, steadily, in our every being
Evidence showing, we are at a good place indeed
No one takes away, or clones, without or within
Creator, Heaven, knows how, in us, He places Heaven
So, not a shame if religion cannot comprehend
Rather, to be proud of talking up learning and serving
For, religion tried what was beyond scope
Blind, unable to lead blind, the quote
So, predestined, not new, to force it, against hope

Deliberate quote, emphasising predestined limitations
Human complexity, desires, ignore this quotation
Bringing us falling flat on our faces, in devastation
The Overall loves us, talking out of love
Not trying to show off, not what He does
So, trying against His word, breaks His Heart

For, He calls the shots, and there is Light
We do not want to be opposite His flight
Because pending devastation, an eternal plight
Yes, laying down Heavenly examples
The only true and righteous sample
Again, The Ultimate Overall, overly ample
In Him, we want to righteously model
For, He alone, The One really dependable
So, in Him, therefore, truly unshakeable
Not just about speeches anymore
But, action, that He explores
Deeds showing clothes we always wore
No time for physically vocal
But, Heavenly displays, truly focal
When in Him, we are indeed, total
Time, demonstrating, message has cut through
Activities, showing faithfully true
Time for trees to bear juicy fruits
Providing for this occasion in all of us
Needing us, moving from minus to plus
To the joy of grateful Heavenly ones
Owe it to ourselves, to be Heavenly inclined

Righteous climb with all the designed
Solution to all woes, as Heavenly destined
Therefore, days of long talk, over
Avenue for days of personal encounter
Off-loading failed targets, assumed, forever
To rewriting "Holy Books", living them, as benchmark
Ensuring levels, are Heavenly standards
From One, who, for our sake, was jeered on placards
Eternal solutions, always, available
Grabbing with both hands, in it, comfortable
He alone, provides answers, sustainable
Clearing into oblivion, the wicked evil reptile
Nabbing our heels, the scoundrel, at domiciles
Becoming witnesses, exposing him, where he occupies
Away with unproductive talk
Production time for bounty stock
Proving, all deadly deeds, stopped
Walking in confidence over deadly mines
Not feeling, were on files
Operating, truly, in new lease of life
Yes, Heavenly trail, to visit
Depicting Him, out of world, with antics
For world, in awe, as epic

Reliving previous glorious dominion
Captivating, not just by human opinion
But, Heaven, in humble reunion
When town-crier conveys lifetime opportunity
Not to be missed, from The Almighty

Chance for each, to regain eternity
Hope none would be apprehensive
For, would prove, very expensive
Push therefore, for achievable goal, decisive
Heaven admitting, very submissive
Courageous in the way, combative
Creating admiration, accreditable, impressive
Non should die empty
Yes, go out on a limb, confidently
Knowing "absolute power corrupts absolutely"
No one should be left in a lurch
Thinking it is the works of church
Should unchurch and Heavenly, search
Be bold, using Heavenly shears
No matter how wet behind the ears
For JESUS always calms fears
Therefore, turning back the hands of time
Believing, up to it, from Heavenly lime
Valuable, quality, Heavenly, our renewed life
So, Heaven calls, to love The Lord thy God
With everything good in one Heavenly accord
Reconciliation, tying us to Eternal Cord
Second, importantly, loving neighbour as self
Importantly, because failures, usually, here
Sin makes identifying Neighbour Saviour, never there
We love calling, Lord, God, all our lives
When He comes in simple human life
We despise Him, evidently, Heavenly, not in line
Weakness, that only He, resolves

Neighbour with updated Heavenly reforms
Key to answers for Heavenly warmth

The Lord The God, very real
Completely overcoming our Achilles heel
Requires Him alone in the deal
Noah typified first earthly destruction then
For, Heaven could not find one sinless here
Who satisfied the terms and conditions laid bare
Hence, NOAH, **N**o **O**ne **A**cknowledges **H**eaven
Truthfully, humanly, him and family finally entered
When all thought his life among men had ended
Days of Sodom and Gomorrah, Lot
Again, Heaven took who He accredited without a dot
The wife, eventually, becoming sad spiritual nought
Apart from Lot and children, Living Omnipotent Truth
No one had Heavenly route
Making a case for Heavenly truce
Thence, from Sodom and Gomorrah
The expansive spread, to all parts, far and wide
Lessons to be learnt, so, with sin do part

SEEK, YE, FIRST, WAS THE HEAVENLY WAR-CRY
FOR ALL, TO HAVE A CEMENTED, HUMBLE LIFE
WE ALL REFUSED HIM, BUT NOW, ASKING, WHY
EVERYONE, SHOULD BE FEARFULLY DEVOTED
TO MOVING FROM ATTRIBUTES, ENDANGERED
FOR, WHAT'S HEAVEN'S RIGHTLY CONSIDERED
SHOULD DO EVERYTHING FASTER ABOUT THIS

FOR, HEAVEN'S WRATH IS ON DECEPTIVE VIMS GET UNASSUMED, EMBRACING HEAVEN'S WITS AWAKE, WORLD, GROUND BENEATH, SINKING

From, the empty to, the wealthy
The, pretty beauty, to, the beast
The very naïve to the conceived
Clear, ignorant, to, the pregnant
The tiny, minor, to, super major
Thence, the innate, to doctorate
Private to Commander-in-Chief
From the victim to the detective
Hence naturalist, to the scientist
Who desires evil's stronghold broken down?
Ensuring his tactics, we crackdown
Eventually off his throne, yes, de-crown
Who is filled with that intention?
Obviously burning with ambition
Yes, in line to forgo inherent inhibitions
Who has embraced Heavenly concept?
No longer to remain spiritually inept
The road to Heaven, readily accept
Not to mention, desirous passion
Honest drive and determination
In harnessed resolution
Desperate for Heavenly fold, our holy grail
Spiritually, mal-nourished, so frail
Needing guide onto Heavenly trail
Therefore, our gracious duty to aspire
From the earthly love, retire

Finally, eternity, rewire
Should, fundamentally, Heavenly, revive
Against evil, rigorously conspire
Daily, in Heavenly breath, respire
Hence, to diligently require
Believing, can never backfire
Heaven, remaining, Ultimate Sapphire

This, never game of risk and reward
Graciously, well-oiled system, best on record
All done, now, bold to report
Having reported, ourselves, we comport
With the only blueprint, for one's comfort
For remaining on sacred concourse
Making Heaven, daily delight
Aware, would be a great bullfight
Regaining rightful birth-right
For, Heavenly inheritance, regifted
Picking up on what's decided
Loss meant defeated
Yes, walking through night without fright
For the chosen, always in His sight
He, in them, chosen, His light
In the night, shines the floodlight
Blazing as required firefight
For He is the ultimate one foresight
He assures, in all honesty
Not a cooked-up fantasy
But, ending, in Heavenly ecstasy
Seriously, we all require

Really seeking the desire
For, Heavenly state to acquire
Strengthening with a lubrication
Best, possible, in His application
Helping preparations to the destination
Yes, expertly, under armour
Possessing assured power
To enter Heavenly empire
Message about long-awaited rapture
Bringing to folks, euphoria
Dream realised, never a chimera
Many talk about rapture
Without understanding how to capture
For leaders translate different adventure
Yes, most fantasise about rapture
Wishful thinking, hoping to avoid torture
But none ably produce the X factor
Rapture, not ordering food from restaurant
Which even requires a few attendants
Delivered at right standards
Rapture starts from A not on X
Not as eating boiled eggs
Or tapping into World Wide Web
Not a feeling, satisfied
Nor offertory, multiplied
Never, the preaching, amplified

Rapture is the Almighty JESUS The Deliverer
Saving, the committed, Heavenly Mediator
Truthful Spirit, in Spirit, He works, The Mentor

So we no longer remain negative Noah
But, by His Grace, living, breathing, "New Knower"
In The Heavenly Truth's seed sower
Humbly anointing individuals duly, world over
Not as the world can savour
Busily discovering, fighting one another
What's already openly manufactured
World claims he discovered, conquered
Joke to who, all sculptured
WUOW, would never know when rapture happening
Remember, He is spirit, thus, operating
Showing, what is within us, emanating
Momentous display of divinity of the highest order
Contrasting, utter foolishness to the wanderer
Who, sadly, assumes is a renowned teacher
Gradual upliftment from world order
For world cannot accept Heavenly fodder
Without enough bite to comprehend, I shudder
Never acquired from religious church
Not when devotion, admired in worldly terms
Forget talks, songs, charities, none worthy, all of them
Religion can never manufacture
Being worse, in truth, than amateur
So much tinnier than miniature
Rapture isn't an event just anyone can culture
No longer for the future
Diligently, would agree with scripture
Acquiring rapture, Heavenly stature
Orderly manufactured from a superstructure
Suffering minute earthly torture

Should do all, to require
The pathway that truly aspire
Heavenly abode, to each inspire
If Heaven descends on earth?
Who knows His worth?
Priceless, Heaven and this world!!!
So, devoted focused deep in tears
Living according to what they hear
In joy and pride their crowns, they wear
The Heavens descended in precious ore
Observing first hand, all human wars
Who can tear down the sinful walls?
Yes, Heaven descended to the humble in awe
Who cannot wait, from The Lord to receive more
The state above all imagination from The Lord

Heaven is screening for what is dear
The world is screaming for what isn't theirs
Who can talk for The Heavens to hear?
Why, rapture would be current feature
Who is looking at the big picture?
Can be grasped with the right nurture
We all need Heavenly restructure
To rightfully acquire Heavenly nature
If, serious about worldly departure
For only Heaven knows right moisture
Correct amount of optimal temperature
To acquire standard structure
No one else has that tincture
Confidently said, at this juncture

To indeed erect right ordained posture
Always, a perfect work of sculpture
Which never suffers permanent misadventure
After, confirmed indelible countersignature
World, screaming for what is not here
Religious people think, Heaven is theirs
We shouldn't delay, to shed eternal tears
For, when Heaven speaks, the devil
When the devil speaks, real angel
How, we're terribly lost in deed
Who has slightest Heavenly brains?
Lifted from sewers, avoiding the drains
Lo, off doomed choo-choo train?
Rapture, a constant in religious lecture
Will always remain, guess work fixture
Following nature of confused mixture
Religion hasn't what it takes for a denture
Let alone a whole Heavenly creature
They cannot foot the humble expenditure
Emphasising on mirage as miracles
Those, unable to understand parables
Are bound to find them truly incredible
Religion doesn't do Heavenly acupuncture
Its deeds, always symbolic of fracture
Without featuring distinct multi-culture
No one boards a plane with a travel card
No one uses an oyster card for a cab
So, religion doesn't manufacture rapture
It is only JESUS who picks us up from endless pit
According to His rare tact and means, to sit

To deliver what even to The Heavens, fits
Heavenly Kingdom inside each, we're told
If I don't develop mine as I grow
Whose then, am I likely to own?

Yes, The Heavenly Kingdom is inside us all
Who then, preaches to The Heavenly Kingdom?
To get any meaningful solution
The Only One who said Heaven is there
Only He knows how to treat this, I declare
Who, our sins, can truly clear!!!
Significant step to the eternal solution
The willingness to forget the past for a revolution
Each, to identify and embrace Heavenly constitution
Yes, The Heavenly Kingdom I should seek first
If in Him, I don't quench my thirst?
Who do I blame should I perform the worst?
My granny may love me so very much
But her ID I cannot touch
For, when Heaven checks, it will just not match
Why, should diligently seek each, own names
We have them, stretch forth limbs to trace
Finally captured, to embrace
For when you run your Heavenly race
Over the biting point, He finds you safe
You can trust Him to keep your own name
As no one uses any other person's
Strictly, about individual focusing, forcing
Identifying and following instructions

Short while, JESUS, apostles, deacons, leave
Who will be a part of the humble tree?
Who partners The Precious Green Leaf?
Green Leaf, and we have the crown
Cannot have one, when dried and down
Hope on the day, no one will frown
JESUS mingled with sinners
We filthy humans, give The Heavens jitters
Who, then, take these to dry cleaners?
When Heaven is refused hearts' entry
Who then enters the sanctuary?
Can only be confirmed obituary
Let us all with one accord
Seek reconciliation with The Heavenly concord
So, ourselves, we can, duly comport
Let us cry onto the Saviour JESUS
Willing to listen, and truly forgive us
Remaking us into quality ordained subjects
Every human being, He is ready to save
Anyone and everyone humble for a name
Heaven confirming, operates without protruding mane
Should all be pushing to make an impression
Good enough for Heaven to see our passion
For JESUS to outstretch arm of compassion

Oh, how sweet is The Lord, The Most High
Who protects His own far and nigh
For whose sake, we heave a relieved sigh
Knowing world full of itself

That is all, it has, to serve
With an indelible eternal curse
But Heaven has renewed our strength
And duly filled us to our depth
Occupying, our length and breadth
Oh, who is like Him?
The unassuming joyful hymn
In whom we can only win !!!
From evil one, He snatched us
Woe unto he, who thinks He is a minus
For, to the wolves, would he be delicious
Our sins, He wants to far away, putt
Just a blink, and humble willing, on His path
Keenly, waiting, to give all, congratulatory pat
Then one thing, though, JESUS asks
That we focus on daily tasks
This way, all conundrums, He surely busts
Yes, the sure thing, from us, He needs
That all become obedient to Him indeed
Humble route, forever cleansing evil deeds
Nothing about verbal prayers
Never to resolve or do us favours
To reach Him obediently, among the players
Prayers, temporarily soothe the desperate!!!
Into feeling, now, everything is, will be okay
But turns out, does not really pay
Why are desperate ones very easy meat?
For those who are supposed to them, feed
Empty them till they can't stand on their feet
While JESUS asks us out of respect

To see how much, to Him, we are honest
How much we dare, He pre-grants our request
Let's take on the challenge, though compelling
For with and in Him, there is no meddling
The hard work finally sees us settling
From intensive care unit to Heavenly stare
Slowly and gradually, He always prepares
To ensure we are finally there

Salvation at Work

Having already spoken about salvation
Now, nine simple words of explanation
From abused, lost, adored, found, recovery, to redemption
Shedding All Load Verily And Transforming Into
Omnipotent Nature
Who has received this Heavenly pager?
WUOW, nothing like world's wager!!!
Sometimes, the saying, "You reap what you sow"
No one works for Tesco
Unknown, let alone, be paid by Costco
"You reap what you sow."
What future are we preparing for the soul?
The measuring of our attitudes says so
Should expect many to budge
Many have qualifications, as shows the badge
But Heavenly trail, not like chocolate fudge
Imagine what racism has done to our lives
Loved ones, who still would've been alive
Could have been enjoying better times

When manufacturer produces billions of cars
And a problem occurs with a car's tyre
Will the manufacturer rejoice after it is done?
No, the manufacturer created all the cars
Fixing a leg, not headline news for joyous cry
But the call to join Heavenly ride
Yeah, difference between, fake and real
Go, show yourself to them, without any more sin
The fake rejoices about what goes in the bin
When Heaven is cleansing unto salvation
Imposter thinks about physical conservation
Therefore, spending years on wasteful preservation
Equipped with Heavenly stance don't brag
Rather, wish, everyone else, they can drag
Avoiding pathetic life, onto Heaven, with a crack
Absolute solution, getting out of death, real fast
Heading for finishing line, to more than pass
Why, nothing about prayers and fasts
But, re-connecting to Heaven effectively
Consistently listening, following directives dutifully
Then, graciously regaining rightful place, accordingly
At some point we realize, cannot do anything
Real lives count for something
Overall costs, we'll be making savings
When we see each as a potential God
We put ourselves on natural forms
Delivering expected divine course
Seeing each other as The God we say we serve
To hurt that person, will require some nerve
Let's walk The Heavenly trail to regain new birth

Seeing each one as The One we passionately cherish
Evidence, on road we don't perish
The Heavenly meal, then, we nourish!!!

A broken heartache, which has been fixed
The journey left us between and be-twitched
Constantly reminding, in world, we could not mix
Helping us endure above duration, golden jubilee
Then, mingling with worldly, with glee
All pleasantries, accordingly, flee
Endured trials, from these worldly hearts
Especially when supposed homes exposed us
Outwardly thinking, we, were so sad
When bandwagons sounded, could not join the carts
Blessedly assuredly, has come to pass!!!
To narrate this story, well into the past
Only The Heavens control own handcarts
Courageously leaving behind worldly cards
Riding joyously, the quality, Heavenly cars
When bandwagons readied, and dealing with pushcarts
Because we've always known it never lasts
Far from preferring the world, with the die, cast
Yes, religion, broken into fragmented pieces
All as one, would make meaningful beginnings
For Heavenly approved sacred eternal finishing
Heavenly religion, indeed, under one umbrella
Not operating like worldly propaganda
Activities fall under one in agenda
Religion will remain, supposed one
Doing what Heaven wants
No longer under the devil's wand

With religion one, each becomes good listener
Practising under Heavenly banner
In a beautifully unique, peaceful, sacred manner
Biggies, including David, never enjoyed worldly religions
Led by Almighty in all regions
Therefore, as having wisdom beyond reason
In their shoes, can we step in truth
Being, brothers and sisters, immune
Heavenly dialogue, we can deduce
When Heaven sends a messenger
The messenger represents the sender
One, we call our creator
Should a ticket be issued by a traffic warden
Parliament punishes the one offending
So, deciding not to pay, never pardoned
Cannot hear from above, peeved
Should not be found in stew
Never a good scene, can only be obscene
Respecting tiny one, high level of love
No one knows, form, The Lord comes
Until after passing initial humility exams

Required terms and conditions
We surrender without inhibitions
As child arrives at best institution
Brethren relied on gracious word
Remembering others also heard
But refused evil, for The Creator instead
Not easy road, needs full commitment
Rough ride, demanding full engagement
One designed with Performance Management

For success requires high performance obligation
Using systems which boast of dynamic innovation
Therefore, victorious with coordinated unification
Heaven provides every required tool
Before we thought, available, for use
Baffling the lot not in tune
Nothing to lose in this matter
Dealing directly, with Ultimate Master
He is real Master Blaster
Blasting away wicked impediments
Freeing us of ill judgments
To stroll in full independence
He decides rulings without hearing from either party
Justified, for in Him, no partiality
Yes, in Him, confidentiality
The one called Mysterious Trust
The vital ingredient missing in world crust
Finding most activities facing irreversible crash
Nothing better than this to have in life
World can walk with creator, Live
Every good, readily filed
Who prepares to put the head where it hurts?
Will manoeuvre peaks and troughs
While managing unwanted strops
Should let go of rampage
For, no reward in this umbrage
Nothing good comes out of this fit of rage

Should throw away deadly irritation
Into the deep, unwanted exasperations
Doing away with perturbation

We need this life of austerity
Choosing to call it severity
Saving grace is Heavenly frugality
Should revert to being Heavenly approved ascetic
Executed constantly in mood, frenetic
World lacking, chosen, unusually pneumatic
Should abandon worldly righteousness
For, not helpful in seriousness
Bearing hallmarks of pure lawlessness
Gradually offloading spell of hypnotism
Under consistently controlled mechanism
Would be free of spellbound plagiarism

The Jew, claims being Heaven's favourite, first
The black man upholds Heaven's physical best
While, white man, maintains, supremacy quest
No peace, truly, because of these, other reasons
Mentioning mildly, money, religious misgivings
Causing a few unsavoury, misguided, misdeeds
We should have buried hatchet by now and fast
For, Heaven expects only quality, humble, casts
To be paraded before The Almighty's elite mass

Let us all, with oneness arise and shine
Heaven is ours, without having to mine
Right within us, pop open, Heavenly wine
We will notice it, tasting better than water
One, we had before, made us stagger
Now, to our senses, in The Master with swagger
All, should, with one accord, laud

Surrendering joyously to The Lord
Who easily reads the heart call
For, world has seen its best days
No longer safe for who, in this, stays
While The Lord has reserved a better place
Let us all, with oneness arise and shine
Heaven has long, had us on the mind
Letting go and tasting Heavenly wine
The JESUS latter wine, better than our water
Making us walk in humble swagger
We thank Him by deeds, The True Master
Who, lucky to be in Heaven's flock?
Does everything to be member of the lot
Wouldn't do anything to desert this anointed block
Religion was never part of Heaven's flock!!!
Why, all they dish out, unwanted blots
Evident about all who sail aboard
His eagle eyes stay on the flock
Who He daily steers onto Heavenly course
Forget everyone's evil concerted plot
Belongs, to the lowly in society flock
Who served everyone, as boss
Worthless in their eyes, as such, tossed
Some would do all to be of this flock
Heaven will ensure they, He, won't block
And to Heaven, finally, would He plod

Who, in right mind would desert this flock?
For everyone has a hole to plug
To narrate own findings as legitimate blog

An honorary honour to be of Heaven's flock
Assuredly concise, always awed
For in humble humility, gladly on all fours
Heaven does not desert His assembled flock
His scope is indeed broad
Unique, this unusual club
This Heavenly ordained blessed flock
Made up of obscurity, yet, gladly plucked
From the brink, have they been clawed
Therefore know nothing outside the flock
For maturity, involving in nothing "gross"
Knowing, every step towards timely clock
Only One Pastor knows the flock
To each, He allocates a semblance of a job
Eventually, nicely in, does each slot
Yes, The Heavenly Pastor knows His flock
For whom He is always on the cross
Graciously, authentically, is each reformed
No one knows better than His flock
Prepared in line with Heavenly form
Who knows he is part of this cohort?
You know when part of flock
Displaying qualities far beyond a flop
When all blots are brought to a halt
Yes Heaven knows His own flock
Among whom there are no frosts
Wherever they are, magnificent, without a
Heaven develops His exemplary flock
So they identify each other's voice
Eternally sealing every obscure void

Heaven has His own flock
In Whom He desires and puts a gloss
As with them, together, they dance the floss
Long live The Heavens and His flock
Though young, JESUS, does pull all stops
Will urge all, to join the bond
"Brevity is the soul of wit"
More to say, but hope this fits
Not to outdo my favoured bit
Concluding, "beware of Greeks bearing gifts"
Smoking out the wily old tricks
Once we focus on eternal Heavenly hints
My JESUS has accredited us with life
With extensive rights
Who can measure the expansive Christ?

We would without You, in. would we not fit
Job on hand, not just a bit
Avoiding bad odour, by Your Grace, we sit
The call joy overrides all
With Your Grace, we did not fall
Assuredly beside us, before thinking of a call
Holding onto our Father, JESUS, The Word
Our Rod and Staff, daily, truly, really cares
Knowing, He will always be alive in this world
We thank You again, Father JESUS, for we can assure
Apostles in Heaven, everyone ensured
Enjoying sweetness on some shores
Who says, for me, should you not weep?
As, this vanishing world, I will not keep

Will blessedly come out of the deep
Rest remains fantastic, glorious history
Because, on course to gracious victory
Won't be blocked by any negative wizardry
Who is ready to say this with action?
Bearing fruits through the right exertions
Catching Heavenly imagination with operations
Apostles, JESUS' Heavenly angels in disguise?
Unlawful treatment, never sorrowful demise
But, with The Heavens, a worthy delight
Being The exemplary Heavenly flute
The Heavens us, re-shapes en-route
To finally play unto all, the best tunes
Heaven's chosen few, He calls sage
Who are prepared to help those requiring aid?
Scattered worldwide, enjoying Heavenly tastes
Treat them Heavenly, to receive some grace
May be The One you pray to, deciding your fate
Beware, one met, could be one who you, would save

Our Honourable Regal Highness
We implore great happiness
To thank You for Your Kindness
You have motivated us to believe
That we can more than achieve
What we set out to receive
The One with The Quality
Which more than describes Your Honesty
We appreciate Your continual innovative Integrity
Inviting us with angels, eternal honour

The kind that comes with bespoke splendour
The opportunity accepted with vigour
Nominated among the elect few, pleasure !!!
Mingling with elite, way beyond measure
Dream inclusion, we will always treasure !!!

Once in a lifetime acquaintance to speak of
Appreciation of the invite, more than enough
Thanks for conquering inhibitions, to ward-off
Who are we, least in society, faces to show?
Perennial outcasts, among your operations to glow
Warmly embraced, for business to flow
Where best could we possibly be?
People would pay huge sums, probably, to steal
Here we are, apostles, poor in spirit, having for free
JESUS, The Only Heavenly approved in Reverence
Yes, the name that has duly earned preference
Accepted in a blink of the eye, as reference
We should come to where if Heaven calls Noah
Not knowing where we are
Under Heavenly interventional arm
Noah should be "New One Acknowledges Heaven"
Opportunity with Heavenly brethren
World, try to be among iconic legends
Excited about meeting the Khalifa,
Will let you know, he also needs The Leader
Someone to assure, he will eternally prosper
The Rabbi knows, others will do all to meet him
But, aware of shortfalls, in unwanted Heavenly din
Consequently, the glowing inner lights, dim

The Bapu has done his ethical bit, too
But acknowledges that Heaven is true
That all need to be replenished anew
For, Life is a Heavenly mission
With Heaven providing cushion
In His eternal vision
Never our intentions
But Heaven's commission
Prevailing for our destination
We adore His provision
Embrace His protection
And His eternal summation

Hence, who dwells secretly in The Most High
Is fed with The Word and sighs
Into The Heavenly Heavens, daily fly
Conforming, not to worldly doxa
Grounded deep in Heavenly quota
Answering calls with chores relative to Heavenly rota
Not like the 'fox set to guard chicken', living
But one with Heavenly splendour, richly pickings
Which only the secret confirm with heartened thanksgiving
Secret, to those it is secret
But Heavenly hearts, remain openly sacred
From continuous cleansing, not done by faces
The Heart of Glorified Father today
Ensuring, children, with Him, in Heaven, stays
From everlasting to everlasting shall all say…

No excitement bigger than meeting JESUS
The Only One, Heavenly standing, for all of us The only one,

Heavenly, standing for all of us
He has done this for some, ready for more others
Then, imagine likes of Moses, Magdalene
Sharing experiences with you, truthfully
Meeting other prophets who performed duties
Awoken to realise, Heaven, better than assumed
So many levels, stages, overly amused
Joy untold in recollecting experiences, bemused
Savouring reality of Who Heaven stands for
A dream no longer, but live, in awesome awe
Never part of my start
To remain a good minor

Then, Personal Thanks to Dream Provider

Your Grace for me is such that
I do not know who enemies are
For You perform all the art
So, when they fall apart
It's not my part of the start
When they fall asunder
Never about when I, recover
For You The Ultimate Deliverer
Prepare my every adventure
When I am deep in slumber
So, every turn I wander
You are already ahead to scatter

Giving me every manna
To remain a good soldier
Not needing other pasture

Oh, Deliverer Messiah
You deserve every Halleluiah
For the timely encounter
Not leaving a second later
Or proactive a second earlier
Your disguise always the matter
For You are The Master
Unto You, I daily surrender
Cleansing without an iota
Of dirt as a sinner
Without even a shiver
For granting more than silver

For You are The Baptiser
Without a competitor
Glory to Humble Saviour
Most Unique Orchestrator
Strategist like no other
Unbelievable Organiser
Our feet in Your Concrete Layer
Assured, never to stagger
So, we stroll with a swagger
For you are the ONE Wonder
Yes, You, are The Alpha
And undoubted Omega

In You, I am a WINNER
With all brethren, TOGETHER
Today and yes, FOREVER

Conclusion

Entering Heaven, costs everyone, this world
Would, however, not cost a dime of this earth
Yes, imperative, getting out of evident dearth
Seek ye first, would have sorted all situations
Realising, we only answer, to one institution
Heaven, guiding humble steps with precision
Born, were introduced to what doesn't matter
Vulnerable, without true, meaningful, answer
Needing salvation, from JESUS, The Creator
So, all should come together brethren, as one
Modestly, burying the hatchet from this mind
Then, averting, what could be otherwise, bad
Humility, oneness, and care, within, brethren
Loving a neighbour, anew daily, as ourselves
To, identify and embrace the one, who serves

Rallied Emotions Leading Ignorant Groups Individual
Onto Nothing (Sacred)
Played important role morally, Great's names, activities,
to behold indeed
Time, though, world moved on to Heavenly
trajectory increase

World's best preaching, fasting, prayers, not Good
Heaven's pleasure
Hence, opportunity rare, to register name in Heavenly Ledger
Believing, someone, world, would hearken to town
crier's gesture
Adhering to offloading everything, worldly postage
Awoken, tasting individual, sacred, encounter dosage
Gingerly, with baby steps, into Heavenly chapter's new cottage
Transformed, from the empty barrel, nuisance, rejected noise
To The Almighty's quality, fruitful, highly esteemed voice
Glorified, from on earth, to The Highest Heaven's, humble poise

HIS OWN PASTOR CHASED HEAVEN'S REALITY
FOR BEING BLASPHEMOUS, YET HE THE DEAL
JOHN THE BAPTIST LED, ETERNALLY, SEALED
PROVES, RELIGIONS BEHIND, TOPMOST ELITE
WITH THE SKINT BECOMING HEAVENLY RICH
ATHEIST, TO THE HEAVEN'S BELOVED ANGEL
NOW, HAVE SUCCOMBED, TO HEAVENLY FIZZ
IN HEAVENLY ORDAINED, DELIGHTFUL, VIMS
THUS, IN EMBRACING, TRUE, HEAVENLY, WITS

REDEEMED WORLD, RELIGION SAVED HUMBLY

HEAVEN'S APPROVED ROADMAP, TO ETERNITY
SHINING LIGHT, INTO CLEAN, SUSTAINABILITY
THANKS, TO THE LOVING, ALMIGHTY'S, GRACE
BECOMING NOW, TRULY HIS CHILDREN, AGAIN
ASSUREDLY, PERFECTLY SECURED INTO PLACE

Thank You, Ultimate Overall, JESUS,
The Only One, Truly, For Us All

References

The Holy Agam Sutras – Jainism
The Holy Avesta – Zoroastrianism
The Holy Bible - Christianity
The Holy Guru Granth Sahib – Sikhism
The Holy Kitab-i-Aqdas – Baha i
The Holy Kojiki – Shinto
The Holy Koran - Islam
The Holy Torah - Judaism
The Holy Tripitaka – Buddhism
The Holy Vedas - Hinduism

Romans, Chapter 3, 9-10

Graciously, by Ernest Brew Obeng
(Obeng, 2021)

www.ingramcontent.com/pod-product-compliance
Lightning Source LLC
Chambersburg PA
CBHW050045120526
44589CB00038B/2727
* 9 7 8 1 8 0 2 2 7 2 4 1 3 *